Nelson Literacy

Senior Author
Jennette MacKenzie

Senior Consultant
Miriam P. Trehearne

Senior Consultant
Carmel Crévola

Series Consultants
Ruth McQuirter Scott—*Word Study*
James Coulter—*Assessment*
Neil Andersen—*Media*
Maureen Innes—*ESL/ELL*
Rod Peturson—*Science*
Nancy Christoffer—*Bias and Equity*

Series Writing Team
Paula S. Goepfert, *Senior Writer*

Marg Camp	Wendy Mathieu
Kathleen Corrigan	Christine McClymont
James Coulter	Heather McGowan
Dianne Dillabough	Bev McMorris
Lalie Harcourt	Thérèse McNamara
Jane Hutchison	Sarah Peterson
Karen Kahler	Liz Powell
Norma Kennedy	Mary Schoones
Christel Kleitsch	Ricki Wortzman

NELSON / EDUCATION

NELSON / EDUCATION

Nelson Literacy 6c
Jennette MacKenzie

Director of Publishing
Kevin Martindale

Director of Publishing, Literacy
Joe Banel

Publisher, Literacy
Rivka Cranley

Executive Managing Editor, Development
Darleen Rotozinski

Senior Product Manager
Mark Cressman

Program Managers
Barbara Hehner
Tracey MacDonald

Project Editor
Lara Caplan

Developmental Editor
David MacDonald

Researchers
Susan Hughes
Catherine Rondina

Assistant Editors
Petal Almeida
Corry Codner

Editorial Assistants
Adam Rennie
Kristen Sanchioni

Executive Director, Content and Media Production
Renate McCloy

Director, Content and Media Production
Carol Martin

Content Production Editor
Christi Davis-Martell

Proofreaders
Jonathan Bocknek
Elizabeth D'Anjou

Production Managers
Cathy Deak
Helen Jager-Locsin

Director, Asset Management Services
Vicki Gould

Design Director
Ken Phipps

Managing Designer
Sasha Moroz

Series Design
Sasha Moroz
Steven Savicky

Series Wordmark
Steven Savicky

Cover Design
Sasha Moroz

Interior Design
Carianne Bauldry
Jarrel Breckon
Brian Cartwright
Claudia Davila
Courtney Hellam
Karin Hincks
Jennifer Laing
Eugene Lo
Sasha Moroz
Roberto Pagliero
Peter Papayanakis
Peggy Rhodes
Jan John Rivera
Studio Montage
Glenn Toddun

Art Buyer
Suzanne Peden

Compositor
Courtney Hellam

Photo Research and Permissions
Lisa Brant
Julie Pratt

Printer
Transcontinental Printing

Advisers and Reviewers: Ontario

Nora Alexander

Stephanie Aubertin, Limestone DSB

Gale Bankowski, Hamilton-Wentworth CDSB

Wendy Bedford, Peterborough Victoria Northumberland and Clarington CDSB

Trudy Bell, Grand Erie DSB

Debra Boddy, Toronto DSB

Maggie Boss, Dufferin-Peel CDSB

Michelle Bryden, Eastern Ontario CDSB

Elizabeth M. Burchat, Renfrew CDSB

Karen Byromshaw, Toronto DSB

Mary Cairo, Toronto CDSB

Cheryl Chapman, Avon Maitland DSB

Cathy Chaput, Wellington CDSB

Christina Clancy, Dufferin-Peel CDSB

Alison Cooke, Grand Erie DSB

Cheryl Cristobal, Dufferin-Peel CDSB

Genevieve Dowson, Hamilton-Wentworth CDSB

Denise Edwards, Toronto DSB

Lorraine Giroux, District School Board of Niagara

Charmaine Graves, Thames Valley DSB

Colleen Hayward, Toronto CDSB

Charmaine Hung, Toronto DSB

Eddie Ing, Toronto DSB

Sue Jackson, Thames Valley DSB

Lee Jones-Imhotep, Toronto DSB

Ray King, Dufferin-Peel CDSB

Tanya Korostil, Peel DSB

Rocky Landon, Limestone DSB

Helen Lavigne, Waterloo CDSB

Luci Lackey, Upper Grand DSB

Laurie Light, Dufferin-Peel CDSB

Lorrie Lowes, Ottawa-Carleton DSB

Maria Makuch, Ottawa-Carleton DSB

Jennifer Mandarino, Dufferin-Peel CDSB

Carolyn March, Hamilton-Wentworth DSB

Mary Marshall, Halton DSB

Claire McDowell, Lambton Kent DSB

Thérèse McNamara, Simcoe County DSB

Andrew Mildenberger, Toronto DSB

Laura Mossey, Durham DSB

Elisena Mycroft, Hamilton-Wentworth DSB

Mary Anne Olah, Toronto DSB

Judy Onody, Toronto CDSB

Eleanor Pardoe, Grand Erie DSB

Krista Pedersen, Upper Canada DSB

Sarah Peterson, Waterloo DSB

Annemarie Petrasek, Huron Perth CDSB

Catherine Pollock, Toronto DSB

Cheryl Potvin, Ottawa-Carleton DSB

Amarjit Rai, Peel DSB

Tara Rajaram-Donaldson, Toronto DSB

Kelly Rilley, Windsor-Essex CDSB

Joanne Saragosa, Toronto CDSB

Katherine Shaw, Peel DSB

Jackie Stafford, Toronto DSB

Elizabeth Taylor, Peel DSB

Sian Thomas, Renfrew DSB

Elizabeth Thompson, Durham DSB

Bonnie Tkac-Feetham, Niagara CDSB

Sandra VandeCamp, Dufferin-Peel CDSB

Ann Varty, Trillium Lakelands DSB

Contents

10

63

75

120

Welcome to
Nelson Literacy

Your *Nelson Literacy* book is full of fascinating stories and articles. Many of the topics are the same as those you will study in science and social studies.

Here are the different kinds of pages you will see in this book:

Let's Talk
Here's a chance to have some fun and also show what you know.

Understanding Strategies
These pages introduce you to reading, writing, speaking, listening, and media literacy strategies. Some pages have sticky notes with hints about the strategies.

Applying Strategies
These pages give you the chance to try out the strategies you've learned.

Putting It All Together
At the end of each unit, you'll have the chance to use the strategies that you've learned.

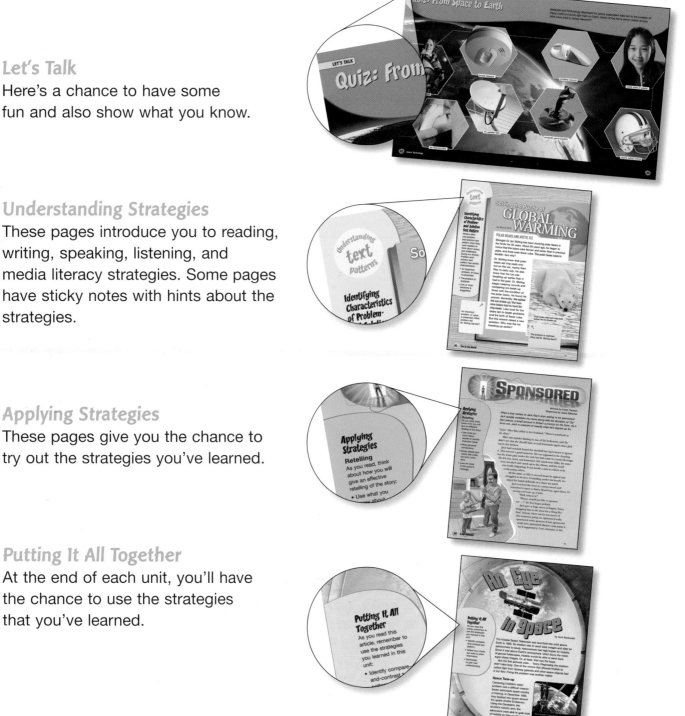

SCIENCE FICTION

In this unit, you will

- identify characteristics of science fiction
- retell stories
- fix run-on sentences in your writing
- evaluate the effectiveness of media texts
- use body language and gestures when speaking

There's No Place Like Home

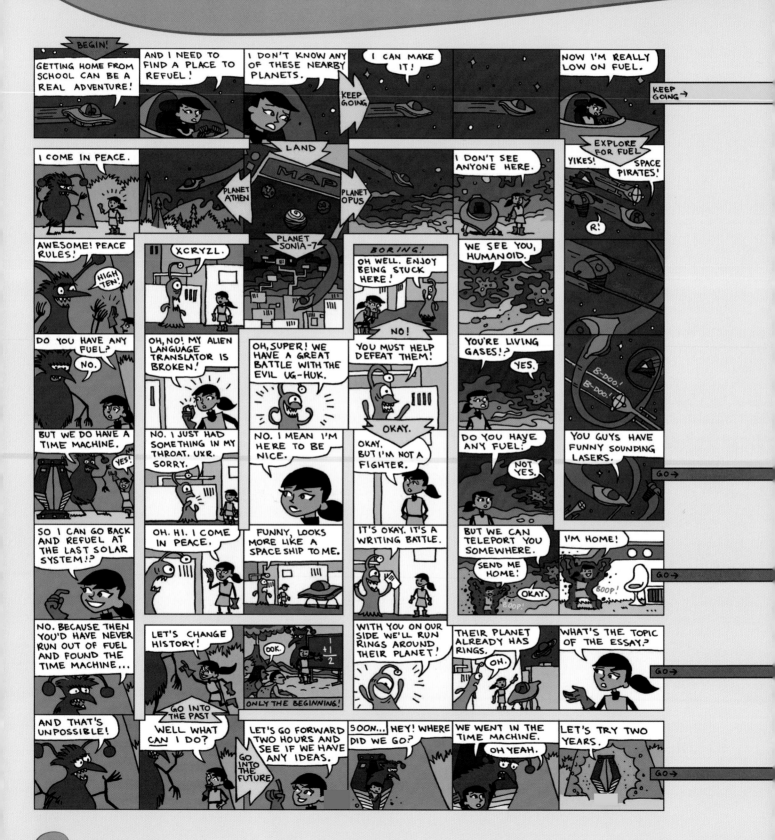

Anything can happen in a science fiction story. Choose different paths through this story to follow Sasha's adventures as she tries to get home from school.

Narrative: Identifying Characteristics of Science Fiction

Science fiction has certain characteristics:

- Science fiction makes predictions about the future.
- Scientific details are often not true—yet.
- Alien characters experience emotions like our own.
- Science fiction can make readers think about today's issues.

THE FUN THEY HAD

Written by Isaac Asimov
Illustrated by Eric Kim

↗

Science fiction makes predictions about the future. What prediction does this story begin with?

Margie even wrote about it that night in her diary. On the page headed May 17, 2155, she wrote, "Today Tommy found a real book!"

It was a very old book. Margie's grandfather once said that when he was a little boy his grandfather told him that there was a time when all stories were printed on paper.

They turned the pages, which were yellow and crinkly, and it was awfully funny to read words that stood still instead of moving the way they were supposed to—on a screen, you know. And then, when they turned back to the page before, it had the same words on it that it had had when they read it the first time.

"Gee," said Tommy, "what a waste. When you're through with the book, you just throw it away, I guess. Our television screen must have had a million books on it and it's good for plenty more. I wouldn't throw *it* away."

"Same with mine," said Margie. She was 11 and hadn't seen as many telebooks as Tommy had. He was 13.

She said, "Where did you find it?"

"In my house." He pointed without looking, because he was busy reading. "In the attic."

"What's it about?"

"School."

↑

Scientific details are often not true—yet. What modern-day technology might replace books entirely?

Margie was scornful. "School? What's there to write about school? I hate school." Margie always hated school, but now she hated it more than ever. The mechanical teacher had been giving her test after test in geography and she had been doing worse and worse until her mother had shaken her head sorrowfully and sent for the County Inspector.

He was a round little man with a red face and a whole box of tools and dials and wires. He smiled at her and gave her an apple, then took the teacher apart. Margie had hoped he wouldn't know how to put it together again, but he knew how all right and, after an hour or so, there it was again, large and black and ugly with a big screen on which all the lessons were shown and the questions were asked. That wasn't so bad. The part she hated most was the slot where she had to put homework and test papers. She always had to write them out in a punch code they made her learn when she was 6 years old, and the mechanical teacher calculated the mark in no time.

The inspector had smiled after he had finished and patted her head. He said to her mother, "It's not the little girl's fault, Mrs. Jones. I think the geography sector was geared a little too quick. Those things happen sometimes. I've slowed it up to an average 10-year level. Actually, the overall pattern of her progress is quite satisfactory." And he patted Margie's head again.

Margie was disappointed. She had been hoping they would take the teacher away altogether. They had once taken Tommy's teacher away for nearly a month because the history sector had blanked out completely.

So she said to Tommy, "Why would anyone write about school?"

← Scientific details are often not true—yet. What modern-day technologies are like Margie's mechanical teacher?

→

Alien characters experience emotions like our own. How are these futuristic friends like kids today?

Tommy looked at her with very superior eyes. "Because it's not our kind of school. This is the old kind of school that they had hundreds and hundreds of years ago." He added loftily, pronouncing the word carefully, "*Centuries* ago."

Margie was hurt. "Well, I don't know what kind of school they had all that time ago." She read the book over his shoulder for a while, then said, "Anyway, they had a teacher."

"Sure they had a teacher, but it wasn't a regular *teacher*. It was a man."

"A man? How could a man be a teacher?"

"Well, he just told the boys and girls things and gave them homework and asked them questions."

"A man isn't smart enough."

"Sure he is. My father knows as much as my teacher."

"He can't. A man can't know as much as a teacher."

"He knows almost as much I betcha."

Margie wasn't prepared to dispute that. She said, "I wouldn't want a strange man in my house to teach me."

Tommy screamed with laughter. "You don't know much, Margie. The teachers didn't live in the house. They had a special building and all the kids went there."

"And all the kids learned the same thing?"

"Sure, if they were the same age."

"But my mother says a teacher has to be adjusted to fit the mind of each boy and girl it teaches and that each kid has to be taught differently."

"Just the same, they didn't do it that way then. If you don't like it, you don't have to read the book."

"I didn't say I didn't like it," Margie said quickly. She wanted to read about those funny schools.

→

Science fiction can make readers think about today's issues. Might computers one day outsmart people? Would that be a problem?

They weren't even half finished when Margie's mother called, "Margie! School!"

Margie looked up. "Not yet, mamma."

"Now," said Mrs. Jones. "And it's probably time for Tommy, too."

Margie said to Tommy, "Can I read the book some more with you after school?"

"Maybe," he said, nonchalantly. He walked away whistling, the dusty old book tucked beneath his arm.

Margie went into the schoolroom. It was right next to her bedroom, and the mechanical teacher was on and waiting for her. It was always on at the same time every day except Saturday and Sunday, because her mother said little girls learned better if they learned at regular hours.

The screen lit up, and it said: "Today's arithmetic lesson is on the addition of proper fractions. Please insert yesterday's homework in the proper slot."

Margie did so with a sigh. She was thinking about the old schools they had when her grandfather's grandfather was a little boy. All the kids from the whole neighbourhood came, laughing and shouting in the schoolyard, sitting together in the schoolroom, going home together at the end of the day. They learned the same things so they could help one another on the homework and talk about it.

And the teachers were people.

The mechanical teacher was flashing on the screen: "When we add the fractions ½ and ¼ ...."

Margie was thinking about how the kids must have loved it in the old days. She was thinking about the fun they had.

> Science fiction can make readers think about today's issues. What thoughts about school did you have while reading this story? ←

THE WATER TRADERS' DREAM

by Robert Priest

Applying Strategies

Narrative: Identifying Characteristics of Science Fiction

As you read, look for these characteristics of science fiction:

- Science fiction makes predictions about the future.
- Scientific details are often not true—yet.
- Alien characters experience emotions like our own.
- Science fiction can make readers think about today's issues.

All the water traders
who trade in outer space
talk of a distant planet—
a magical, mystical place
that has seas and seas full of water,
sweet water beyond all worth.
They say that planet is green in the sun
and the name of that planet is Earth.

And the people there drink the water,
they dive and swim in it too.
It falls from the sky in water storms
and it comes in the morning as dew.
That sweet, sweet water is everywhere—
Sweet water! Sweet water of Earth!
And the traders say that the people there
have no idea what it's worth.

So the traders have their earth dreams.
They dream of one silver cup
brought back across space from the earthlings
for millions to drink it up.
"Sweet water! Sweet water! Sweet water of Earth!
The people there trade it for gold!
They've no idea what water's worth—
just look how much they've sold!"

They dream the dream of a water storm—
surely it would drive one mad
to have a wind-full of water flung in your face,
to sail in it like Sinbad!
Yes, they say there are whole oceans there
where waves break on the shore,
where winds leave water singing
and the sunlight makes it roar!

They say that those who live there
just don't know its true worth.
They say that planet is green in the sun
and the people there call it the Earth.

Reflect on

Strategies: How do you know that this is a science fiction poem? Which characteristic of science fiction do you think most strongly matches the poem?

Connections: Where else have you read or heard that water is a valuable resource? How did this knowledge help you understand the poem?

They're Made out of Meat

A one-act play by Terry Bisson

The set is a deep space galactic panorama projected on a screen—the Universe. Two lights moving like fireflies among the stars on the screen represent the Two Voices.

Voice One: They're made out of meat.

Voice Two: Meat?

Voice One: Meat. They're made out of meat.

Voice Two: Meat?

Voice One: There's no doubt about it. We took several aboard our recon vessels from different parts of the planet and probed them all the way through. They're completely meat.

Voice Two: That's impossible. What about the radio signals? The messages to the stars?

Voice One: They use the radio waves to talk, but the signals don't come from them. The signals come from machines.

Voice Two: So who made the machines? That's who we want to contact.

Voice One: *They* made the machines. That's what I'm trying to tell you. Meat made the machines.

Voice Two: That's ridiculous. How can meat make a machine? You're asking me to believe in sentient meat.

Voice One: I'm not asking you, I'm telling you. These creatures are the only sentient race in that sector and they're made out of meat.

Voice Two: Maybe they're like the orfolei. You know, a carbon-based intelligence that goes through a meat stage.

Voice One: Nope. They're born meat and they die meat. We studied them for several of their lifespans, which didn't take long. Do you have any idea what's the lifespan of meat?

Voice Two: Spare me. Okay, maybe they're only part meat. You know, like the weddilei. A meat head with an electron plasma brain inside.

Applying Strategies

Narrative: Identifying Characteristics of Science Fiction

As you read, look for these characteristics of science fiction:

- Science fiction makes predictions about the future.
- Scientific details are often not true—yet.
- Alien characters experience emotions like our own.
- Science fiction can make readers think about today's issues.

Voice One: Nope. We thought of that, since they do have meat heads, like the weddilei. But I told you, we probed them all the way through.

Voice Two: No brain?

Voice One: Oh, there's a brain all right. It's just that the brain is *made out of meat!* That's what I've been trying to tell you.

Voice Two: So...what does the thinking?

Voice One: You're not getting it, are you? You're refusing to deal with what I'm telling you. The brain does the thinking. The meat.

Voice Two: Thinking meat! You're asking me to believe in thinking meat!

Voice One: Yes, thinking meat! Conscious meat! Loving meat. Dreaming meat. The meat is the whole deal! Are you beginning to get the picture or do I have to start all over?

Voice Two: Omigosh. You're serious then. They're made out of meat.

Voice One: Thank you. Finally. Yes. They are indeed made out of meat. And they've been trying to get in touch with us for almost a hundred of their years.

Voice Two: Omigosh. So what does this meat have in mind?

Voice One: First it wants to talk to us. Then I imagine it wants to explore the Universe, contact other sentiences, communicate, swap ideas and information. The usual.

Voice Two: We're supposed to talk to meat.

Voice One: That's the idea. That's the message they're sending out by radio. "Hello. Anyone out there? Anybody home?" That sort of thing.

Voice Two: They actually do talk, then. They use words, ideas, concepts?

Voice One: Oh, yes. Except they do it with meat.

Voice Two: I thought you just told me they used radio.

Voice One: They do, but what do you think is *on* the radio? Meat sounds. You know how when you slap or flap meat, it makes a noise? They talk by flapping their meat at each other. They can even sing by squirting air through their meat.

Voice Two: Omigosh. Singing meat. This is altogether too much. So what do you advise?

Voice One: Officially or unofficially?

Voice Two: Both.

Voice One: Officially, we are required to contact, welcome, and log in any and all sentient races or multibeings in this quadrant of the Universe, without prejudice, fear, or favour. Unofficially, we advise that we erase the records and forget the whole thing.

Voice Two: I was hoping you would say that.

Voice One: It seems harsh, but there is a limit. Do we really want to make contact with meat?

Voice Two: I agree 100 percent. What's there to say? "Hello, meat. How's it going?" But will this work? How many planets are we dealing with here?

Voice One: Just one. They can travel to other planets in special meat containers, but they can't live on them. And being meat, they are limited to the speed of light, which makes the possibility of their ever making contact pretty slim. Infinitesimal, in fact.

Voice Two: So we just pretend there's no one home in the Universe.

Voice One: That's it.

Voice Two: Cruel. But you said it yourself, who wants to meet meat? But the ones who have been aboard our vessels, the ones you probed? You're sure they won't remember?

Voice One: They'll be considered crackpots if they do. We went into their heads and smoothed out their meat so that we're just a dream to them.

Voice Two: A dream to meat! How strangely appropriate, that we should be meat's dream.

Voice One: And we marked the entire sector "unoccupied."

Voice Two: Good. Agreed, officially and unofficially. Case closed. Any others? Anyone interesting on that side of the galaxy?

Voice One: Yes, a rather shy but sweet hydrogen core cluster intelligence in a class nine star in G445 zone. Was in contact two galactic rotations ago, wants to be friendly again.

Voice Two: They always come around.

Voice One: And why not? Imagine how unbearably, how unutterably cold the Universe would be if one were all alone....

Reflect on

Strategies: How do you know that this is a science fiction story? Which characteristic of science fiction do you think most strongly matches the story?

Connections: What other stories have you read or watched where characters have negative attitudes to others because they are different? Try to think of fiction and nonfiction examples.

Fixing Run-on Sentences

Think of a time when you were listening to someone and had to stop the speaker to say, "Slow down!" When someone is talking very quickly, sentences run together and listeners get lost.

The same thing can happen when you are writing. Readers, like listeners, need pauses and breaks to help them see where one idea ends and another begins.

When this writer was revising her science fiction story, she found three run-on sentences.

> **Use a conjunction, such as or, and, or but, to join two complete sentences.**

A massive explosion rocked Canadat, **but** stabilizers steadied the spaceship instantly.

Maxim didn't panic; stabilizers always worked.

> **Use a semicolon to join two short, closely related sentences.**

> **Use a period, question mark, or exclamation mark to end complete sentences. Begin new sentences with a capital letter.**

The captain was barking orders to strike back. six Hornet aircraft prepared to launch. would the captain let Maxim pilot the lead aircraft this time?

How to fix run-on sentences:

☑ Read your writing out loud. Pause only when you see a comma, semicolon, or end punctuation.

☑ Identify any run-on sentences.

☑ Join complete sentences by adding a conjunction or a semicolon.

☑ End complete sentences with a period, question mark, or exclamation mark.

You Be the Judge

Evaluating Back Covers of Books

There's an old saying: "You can't judge a book by its cover." Yet many readers use the back covers of books to help them decide what to read. Are back covers good decision-making tools? You need to answer that question one book at a time by evaluating how effectively the information and ideas are presented.

A back cover often tries to provide evidence that the book will deliver great reading. What evidence do you find on this back cover? How convincing do you find the evidence?

A back cover often gives information about the story in a way designed to make readers want to read more. How effectively does this information draw you into the book?

A back cover has strong word choices to help readers make connections with the book. How effectively do the words on this back cover connect to your reading interests?

"full of menace, mystery and marvels, freewalker is a compelling read made even better by dennis foon's ability to combine great fantasy and sf ideas."
—garth nix

In this evocative, mythic, and powerful second novel in *The Longlight Legacy*, Dennis Foon again displays his great originality and unstoppable imagination.

One year has passed since Roan, Alandra, and the children escaped from the Brothers. The children have begun traveling the Dreamfield with Alandra, but when they fall into a life-threatening coma, Roan and Lumpy set off to find a cure. Roan's lost sister, Stowe, may be the key. But Stowe, now the icon of the City, has become obsessed with her growing powers—powers that threaten to overwhelm her.

Chilling and suspenseful, Foon delivers unexpected twists as he continues his riveting tale.

CRITICAL PRAISE FOR **the dirt eaters**:

★ VOYA's Fantasy, Science-Fiction and Horror Honor List
★ "The Year's Best" 2003 List, Resource Links
★ New York Public Library *Books for Teens List*

"This outstanding first title in a trilogy should have readers eagerly anticipating the next installment."
—*School Library Journal*, starred review

"Junior and senior fantasy fans… will wait impatiently for the next two volumes."
—*VOYA*

$9.95 U.S. / $12.95 CDN
ISBN 1-55037-884-8
Annick Press
www.annickpress.com

You be the judge of this back cover. Look for evidence that the book will be good reading. Decide how effective the information and word choices are at making you want to read the book.

do the same thing for pg 20

It's the world of the future—turned inside out, beyond anything you have ever imagined . . .

ZIMBABWE, 2194: General Matsika's three children steal out of the house on a forbidden adventure—and disappear. Their parents call in Africa's most unusual detectives: the Ear, the Eye and the Arm. Their mission takes them from the underbelly of the city to the swaying top of the Mile-High MacIlwaine Hotel. Yet the children stay just out of their reach. The evils of the past, the technology of the future, criminals with plans far beyond what anyone can imagine—can the Matsika children escape from the heart of it all?

"A marvelous odyssey featuring a witty projection of the future, a score of vividly realized characters, and a nonstop adventure that's at once taut, comic, and touching. Just right to pair with Lois Lowry's *The Giver*."

—*Kirkus Reviews*, pointer review

ALSO BY
NANCY FARMER
Do You Know Me

Cover illustration copyright
© Broeck Steadman, 1995
Cover design by Deborah Kaplan

A PUFFIN BOOK
U.S. $6.99
CAN. $9.99

1014

0-14-037641-0   37641>

UPC

0 51488 00699 2

VISIT US AT www.penguinputnam.com

Using Body Language and Gestures

Your body is a powerful communication tool. You can let people know you are surprised, thrilled, or bored without saying a word.

When you want to use your body to help you communicate your message to an audience, it's a good idea to think about your body language and plan your gestures in the same way that you plan your ideas and your expressions.

This boy is using a mirror to practise his speech on the search for extraterrestrials. Notice how he uses body language and gestures to match his words.

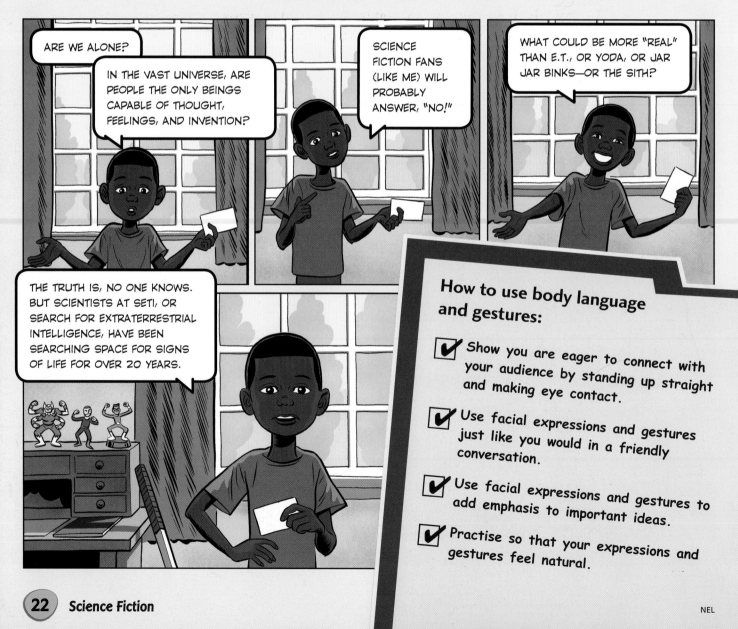

How to use body language and gestures:

☑ Show you are eager to connect with your audience by standing up straight and making eye contact.

☑ Use facial expressions and gestures just like you would in a friendly conversation.

☑ Use facial expressions and gestures to add emphasis to important ideas.

☑ Practise so that your expressions and gestures feel natural.

Retelling

Retelling is a good strategy for helping you deepen your understanding of a story. As you read, watch for important ideas. Combine these ideas to give an effective retelling of the story.

LiTTLE GREEN MEN

Written by Barry B. Longyear
Illustrated by Dave Kang

Use what you know about stories to identify important ideas. What have you learned about the setting and characters in this story? What kind of story is it?

Use what you know about stories to identify important ideas. What is the problem in this story?

Jhanni caught his breath and rested in the shade of a boulder; he had found nothing. His father had forbidden him to search with the other Star Scouts for the UFO reported three days ago, and he wouldn't think of disobeying his father. Still, I said nothing about searching on my own, thought Jhanni.

"All this about 'invaders from outer space' is nonsense." His father had been unshakable on the subject, and nearly everybody thought the same way since the probe to Venus had reported no detectable life on the planet. *Adventurer 7* had met with a mishap on its way to Saturn, and Jhanni's father had been furious. "More taxpayers' money thrown away on foolishness! We should spend the money to take care of problems here." Evidently the government felt the same way. When Jhanni turned 13, the space program was cancelled. Along with the program, the Star Scouts were officially scrapped.

Still, Jhanni's friends, and Star Scouts from all over, kept their squadrons alive to search for evidence—proof that would rekindle the space program and put them back on their road to the stars. Every time a UFO was reported, the squadron in that area would turn out and search for evidence—disturbed soil, burn marks, abandoned equipment—anything. But two years of searching had turned up nothing.

"Someday," Jhanni had told his squadron, "someday we'll find the proof we need, but until then we have to keep on trying." Nevertheless, one by one, the Star Scouts were leaving the squadron. Some, like Jhanni, were forbidden to waste good study time on such foolishness; others were discouraged; and still more had come to believe as their parents believed: Space travel costs too much to spend for uncertain returns. Jhanni's father had pulled him out of the squadron when his grades began to drop.

→

Make personal connections. When have you and your parents disagreed about something important?

"We've had UFO reports for years. Spaceships, death rays, and little green men from outer space, and it's always been something that could be explained. I don't want you ruining your education by wasting your time with it."

Jhanni loved his father, but he had argued with him for the first time in his life. "How do you know there's no life on other planets? Isn't it possible?"

"No one knows for sure, Jhanni, but I'll tell you this: Before I believe it, someone's going to have to show me one of those little green men."

And that's what we're looking for, thought Jhanni, one of those little green men. He pushed away from the boulder and stepped into the sunlight. Shielding his eyes, he looked around. The squadron was searching the hills north of the development where the "object" was reported to have come down during the dust storm three days ago. His father wouldn't give his permission to join the search in the hills, and Jhanni was so angry it took him three tries to properly cycle the airlock on his home before stepping out into the desert.

He went south from the development to search the boulder field, although the "object" was reported north. The windstorm was blowing south that day, thought Jhanni. It's possible; not probable, but possible.

→

Notice details and words that make the story come alive. Which details and words could you include in your retelling?

→

As he looked out over the boulder-strewn desert floor, the evening shadows grew long. Soon it would be dark and the desert cold. He checked the light buckle and heater in his belt and headed for his favourite boulder. At every turn he strained to glimpse the spaceship he hoped would be there. He knew he could get a better view from his boulder, the largest one in the field. It was pockmarked with great holes bored there by the action of the wind and sand, and Jhanni hadn't been there since he was a child playing with the friends who later became his mates in the Star Scouts.

Sometimes he would take one of his mother's blankets and some extra power cells and spend most of an icy night on his boulder, looking at the stars and dreaming of travelling among them. But the dreams became fewer as he grew older. There was no official interest anymore in moons, planets, stars, or anything else that might cost the taxpayers more money.

As the sun dropped below the horizon, the stars appeared, and Jhanni watched them as he reached his boulder and climbed to the top. As he watched the countless pinpricks of light from unknown and unexplored stars, he let himself dream again of flying among them. His eyes glistened and he looked down. Maybe it is childish, he thought. The road to the stars is closed unless people can see the little green men in the flesh. And maybe … maybe the little green men don't exist after all.

Jhanni thought he heard a sound, and he looked over his shoulder. Seeing nothing unusual, he crawled over and around the boulder, looking into the tiny, windblown caves. There was nothing. He shrugged and stood atop the boulder, looking toward the development and his home. The outside light was on at his house, and his mother would scold him if he was late for dinner. He shook his head when he remembered he still had a tough stretch of homework to do and a math test in the morning. He knew he'd better pass this one. Too much imagination and not enough perspiration, his father would say if he failed. Taking one last look at the stars, Jhanni sighed and began to climb down from the boulder.

PING.

Jhanni froze. Slowly he turned his head in the direction of the sound. Deep in the shadow of a wind hole, a tiny light danced back and forth. Warily he crept toward the hole.

Look for clues to the author's message. What do you think the author wants to say about space exploration?

←

←

Use what you know about stories to identify important ideas. What might be the turning point in the story?

"HEY!"

Jhanni picked himself off the ground, knocked there by the suddenness of the sound. He reached to his belt and turned on his light buckle, aiming it at the hole. Inside there was a small, white cylinder propped up on spindly legs supported by round pads. The cylinder was dented, and its legs looked bent and battered.

"Turn off the light! I can't see."

Jhanni turned off his light buckle, and as his widening eyes adjusted again to the dark, tiny lights on the cylinder appeared and illuminated the hole. On one side of the object a tiny door opened, and a small, white-clad creature emerged, looked around, and climbed down a tiny built-in ladder to the bottom of the wind hole. Jhanni peered closely as the creature lifted something and aimed it in Jhanni's direction.

"Can you hear me?"

"Uh...."

"Hold it." The creature adjusted a knob on its chest. "Had to lower the volume a bit. Good thing you dropped by; I only have a day's life-support left."

"Uh …" Jhanni tried to untie his tongue, a million questions in his mind competing for the first answer. "Are you … are you from up there?" He pointed up. "How can you talk to me, and where …?"

"One thing at a time. That's where I come from, and I'm talking to you through a universal translator. I rigged it up with a speaker from the lander console in case anyone came by."

"What happened?"

The creature threw up its tiny arms. "What didn't? I've been out of touch with my base ever since the wind blew me into this hole three days ago, damaging my oxygen regulator and radio. I'm running a little short. Can you get me to an oxygen-enriched atmosphere?"

→ Use what you know about stories to identify important ideas. What event would you be sure to include in your retelling?

"Well … there's my gas box. I raise tropical insects, and they're oxygen absorbing. I did it for a school project in biochem once, and...."

"Do the bugs eat meat?"

"Oh. Well, I can put them in another container. Can you fly or anything? My home's quite a walk from here."

"I guess you better carry me, but take it easy."

"I will." Jhanni picked up the little creature and held it in his hand, surprised at its weight. It was only as tall as one of Jhanni's fingers. He could just barely see the creature shaking his head inside his tiny helmet.

"I can't get over how big you Martians are. Wait until Houston hears about this!"

Jhanni laughed. "If you think I'm big, wait until you see my father!" And wait until my father gets a load of you, thought Jhanni. "By the way, creature, what colour are you under that suit?"

"My name's Frank Gambino, Captain, United States Air Force. I'm sort of brown; why?"

"No special reason." Jhanni slipped the tiny creature into his pocket and began climbing down from the boulder. The little man isn't green, thought Jhanni, but he'll do. As he reached the desert floor and started to run home, he stopped himself just in time from patting his pocket.

Look for clues to the author's message. What do you think the author wants to say about the idea that humans are not alone in the universe?

SPONSORED

Written by Hazel Townson
Illustrated by Jason Edmiston

23 ideas
for each page

Applying Strategies

Retelling

As you read, think about how you will give an effective retelling of the story:

- Use what you know about stories to identify important ideas.

- Make personal connections.

- Notice details and words that make the story come alive.

- Look for clues to the author's message.

When a boy comes to Jack Ray's door asking to be sponsored, Jack quickly scribbles his name along with his donation of "2p" (two pence, a small amount in British currency) on the form. As it turns out, Jack is unaware of exactly what he's signed up for.

"Jack?" Alice Ray called to her husband. "There's somebody at the door."

Alice was upstairs dusting in one of the bedrooms, and she didn't see why she should have to trail downstairs again when Jack was in the kitchen.

Jack had certainly heard the doorbell but had chosen to ignore it. This was not a good moment. He was supposed to be cleaning out the waste pipe under the sink but had come to a nasty blockage. He felt hot, tired, and frustrated. His hands were filthy, his arms were streaked with muck up to the elbows, and the smell was totally disgusting. It was hardly a state in which to be confronting callers.

All the same, at Alice's second shout he sighed and struggled to his feet. Grumbling under his breath, he wiped his hands defiantly on a clean tea towel.

Jack reached the door in a mean mood and wrenched it open to find a blond boy, aged about 10, staring solemnly up at him.

"Well, what is it?"

"Please, would you like to sponsor me …?" the boy began politely.

Jack gave a huge snort of disgust. Fancy dragging him to the door for a thing like that! Anyway, there was far too much of this nonsense going on. Sponsored walk; sponsored swim; sponsored fast; sponsored read; even sponsored silence—you name it, he'd supported it. Cost a fortune, it did.

He felt like slamming the door in the boy's face. But then he realized that this might well be one of his own children's friends—a classmate of Robert's or a brother of one of Emily's cronies. The lad was about their age.

Grudgingly, Jack took the proffered clipboard and scribbled his name where the boy showed him.

"Kids!" he was thinking, "Always wanting something. Never satisfied, our two included!"

The boy checked the signature, then wandered off, apparently quite satisfied. Jack started back to the kitchen.

Alice leaned over the banister rail.

"Who was it, then?"

"Oh, only some kid wanting sponsoring. Blessed pests, they are."

"Sponsoring for what?"

"I dunno!"

"Well, why didn't you ask?"

"He'll tell us when he comes for his money!"

Several days passed before the blond boy called again. This time he had a girl with him, equally blond but slightly smaller than himself. The two of them were so alike that she must obviously be his sister, if not his twin.

Jack answered the door again, in a better mood this time. He recognized the boy at once.

"Oh, it's you!"

He began searching his pockets for some money.

"What's the damage, then?" he asked.

The boy gave Jack the full force of his solemn stare.

"No damage," he replied politely, "Unless you break the agreement, of course. It's up to you."

"What?"

Jack was outraged. He paused with his fist full of coins and scowled at the boy.

"Now, look here!" he said sternly, "You can't go around talking to people like that. You'll end up in a lot of trouble...."

But before he could say any more, the boy took hold of the girl's hand and began to draw her into the house. Together they pushed their way firmly past Jack and advanced down the hall toward the kitchen.

Jack could not believe his eyes.

"Where do you think you're going?"

The odd thing was that Jack suddenly felt afraid. Afraid of two young children, no older than his own pair! What was the matter with him? He should have stopped their progress, but he didn't. He simply stood there staring after them as they approached the kitchen.

Suddenly the kitchen door flew open and Alice's head appeared. "Now what's going on?"

Alice had been baking lemon buns for her children to eat with their glass of milk when they came in from school, and a warm, delicious smell spread through the hall.

"Oh—hello!" Alice was surprised to see the boy and girl, but assumed they must be friends of her children.

"Come to play, have you? You're a bit early. Robert and Emily aren't home yet. They'll be another quarter of an hour or so."

Obviously these two went to a different school which finished earlier.

"I am Robert and this is Emily," the boy announced solemnly in what Alice took to be a slightly foreign accent.

Alice giggled uneasily. "Well, fancy that. There's a coincidence then."

She stared in growing bewilderment at the two children, knowing quite well she had not seen them before. Nobody could forget such unusual features.

The girl pushed past Alice and began to walk round the kitchen, examining everything with great interest. At last she said, "I think we shall like it here, Robert."

"Of course we shall, Emily. It's what we've always wanted." The boy walked over to the refrigerator and opened it, smiling at the contents.

The girl turned to Alice.

"No reason why we shouldn't get on. You will soon grow used to us."

Then the boy sat down on Robert's chair and turned to Jack.

"It would have been quite in order for you just to sponsor me," he said, "but you wrote '2p' which we took to mean 'two people,' so I brought my sister along as well. Anyhow, it will be better this way, two of a kind under the same roof. We can work together. What is it you say?— two heads are better than one?"

Alice stared wildly at Jack. "What are they on about?" She suddenly realized she felt deathly cold, despite her afternoon in the hot kitchen.

Wide-eyed, Jack slowly shook his head, unable to speak a word.

The girl now sat down in Emily's place at the kitchen table and reached for a bun, while the boy picked up Robert's glass and began drinking his milk.

At last Jack pulled himself together. In a voice that sounded strangely shrill he cried:

"Now look here, who the dickens do you think you are, marching into our kitchen as if you owned the place …?"

Solemn as ever, the boy replied:

"But we do own the place. We belong here now. You did not give me time to explain when I first called. You seemed very eager to sign and be gone. But you must have realized what you were taking on. It was written in two languages on the form. We are YOUR children now. You sponsored us for a life on Earth."

Alice gave a cry as her hand flew to her mouth.

"Jack …?"

For a moment she stood rigid with horror. Then true panic took hold as she shrieked:

"Where are our two? Our Robert and Emily—where are they?"

Even as she spoke, there came a mighty rushing sound from the field behind the house and a circular silver object, dazzling and immense, spun off into space at almost the speed of light.

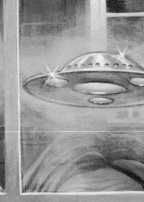

Reflect on

Strategies: How did thinking about retelling the story help you to deepen your understanding?

Critical Literacy: How might this story be different if the author's message was that aliens—when we meet them!—will be friendly, peaceful participants in life on Earth?

A WORLD OF DIFFERENCE

Written by Eric Brown
Illustrated by Rob Fiore

Suzie N'Dah found the alien in Safeway, down the frozen food aisle. She didn't know that the alien was an alien at first. She thought it was a girl, just like herself.

Kim Reed and a couple of her friends had chased Suzie through the small market town, shouting that they were going to beat her up.

Suzie ran like the wind. Her ice-skating practice had improved her running, making her fit and fast. She dashed into Safeway, hurried down an aisle, and hid behind a stack of baked beans. When she peered round the corner and through the window, she saw the tall figure of Kim leading the others past the supermarket and across the cobbled town square. She sighed with relief. All day at school Kim had threatened to get her, and at the final bell Suzie had run from the classroom and never stopped.

It was Friday now. She had a whole weekend free from Kim to look forward to.

Suzie walked down the aisle to the exit, and then she saw the girl.

She was thin and pale, dressed in a dirty pink sweater and jeans too small for her. What made Suzie notice her was not her thin face or her poor clothing, but what she was doing. The girl had her hands thrust into the refrigerator, clutching a family-sized tub of raspberry-ripple ice cream as if frozen in the process of lifting it out.

Suzie told herself that she should ignore the girl, walk past her, and go home. But the girl looked ill. She was breathing deeply, and her face was covered in beads of sweat.

Suzie stopped beside her. "Are you okay?"

The girl turned her head, slowly. She blinked her big blue eyes, staring at Suzie without a word. Suzie guessed that she was 10 or 11.

"I said, are you okay? You'll get frostbite if you don't let go."

The girl just stared, her thin face sickly pale.

"What's your name?" Suzie asked. "I haven't seen you around here before."

The girl moved her lips, and a tiny voice said, "Help me."

The request alarmed Suzie. She looked around to see if anyone was watching.

"What's wrong with you?"

"I'm too hot. I need the cold. Help me!"

"You've got a temperature—a fever. Wait here. I'll go and get a doctor."

"No!" the girl hissed. "Not a doctor. I need a cold place, and then I will be okay."

Suzie could not help laughing. "Is that why you're holding the ice cream?"

The girl nodded. "That is why I am holding the ice cream," she said. "To lower my body temperature to that which I am more accustomed."

Suzie blinked. The girl's speech became more complicated with every sentence she spoke. *Weird....*

"Who are you?" Suzie asked.

"My name is ..." and the girl said a word that sounded like *Fay*. "Please help me. I am too hot and am in danger of expiring—"

Expiring.... The word sounded odd, coming from the mouth of the scruffy 10-year-old.

"Okay, Fay. Tell me where you live. I'll take you home."

"You cannot take me home. That is impossible. I need conditions where the ambient temperature is close to zero. Then I will no longer be in danger. Can you help me?"

There was something seriously weird about the girl, her need for cold, and her strange speech. Suzie wanted to back away, not get involved, but at the same time there was no doubting that Fay needed her help.

"*Please*," said the girl.

"Okay," Suzie said. "I know somewhere. Come with me."

Fay dropped the tub of ice cream and followed Suzie from the supermarket, her short legs moving stiffly. Outside the automatic doors, Suzie grabbed Fay's sleeve.

"What?" Fay asked.

"Not so fast. Kim and her friends are after me. If they see me now...."

Fay looked at her. "You have enemies?"

"I've never thought of them as *enemies*," Suzie said. "But I suppose you could call them that."

"Why do they wish you harm?"

Suzie scanned the cobbled square. There was no sign of Kim or the others. She turned to Fay. "Because of this," she said, pointing to her skin. "They are white and I'm black."

Fay blinked. "In this country people are antagonistic toward others of difference?"

Suzie laughed. "You could put it like that," she said. "Where have you been all your life? Come on, follow me."

They crossed town and headed for the skating rink.

· · ·

"Don't be scared. Just go easy at first, okay? Hold on to the rail until you feel confident enough to let go."

She helped Fay onto the ice. The girl clutched the rails and knelt, laying a palm flat on the surface of the wet ice. An expression of bliss crossed her face. Suzie was glad that there was no one else on the rink to witness the girl's strange behaviour.

"Cold enough for you?" Suzie asked.

"For the time being, it will be okay. How long can I remain in this building?"

"Well...."

Last year, after evening skating practice, Suzie had fallen asleep in the seats overlooking the rink. She had awoken in darkness, wondering where she was. Then she'd remembered, and panicked. Luckily a security guard had heard her cries, found her, and phoned her father.

"You can stay all night if you want," Suzie said. "I'll show you … if you tell me who you are and where you're from."

Fay looked at her. "I am from another country, a cold place—"

"The Arctic?"

The girl nodded.

"How did you get here?"

"How else? I flew."

"Okay. Silly question." Suzie shook her head, exasperated. "Look, I'm not stupid. Even Inuit don't like the cold like you do. They wear thick coats to protect themselves. You—" she looked at Fay's hands, flat on the ice—"you seem to *need* the cold."

The girl stared at Suzie, her big blue eyes unblinking, and then looked away.

Later, when Suzie had done a few practice laps, she took Fay into the darkened seats high above the rink. "Stay here. Hide behind the seats. In a few hours they'll turn the lights out. Then you can go down to the ice again. I'll come and see you tomorrow, okay?"

Fay nodded.

Suzie stared at the girl in the shadows. In the hour she had been with Fay, the strange girl had changed. She looked taller now, and not as thin. And—but surely Suzie was imagining this—her skin was no longer deathly pale, but almost bronzed.

She said a hurried goodbye to Fay and quickly left the building.

· · ·

Suzie ate supper with her mother and father. The TV muttered in the corner of the room. "You were late home tonight, Sue," her mother said.

"I went to the rink."

"I don't like you staying out so late."

Suzie stared at her mother. "I was *practising*. You go on about how I should always practise, and then when I do. …"

Her father shushed them. "Listen—news about the meteor."

"What meteor?" Suzie asked.

"Listen, and you'll find out." He turned up the sound.

Suzie watched the report. Last night a meteor had crashed to Earth a kilometre outside town, landing in a farmer's field and setting fire to the crop of wheat. The pictures showed a blackened field, a deep crater cordoned off by tape, and police standing guard. The reporter said that several eyewitnesses had seen the fiery ball hurtling through the sky, and he went on to say that the authorities denied that the object was a UFO.

Suzie woke at eight in the morning, pulled on her black leggings and orange sweatshirt.

She remembered that it was Saturday—no school. She would go to the skating rink, meet Fay, and this time find out the truth about the strange, cold-loving girl.

• • •

"Fay? Fay, where are you?"

Suzie carried her skates over her shoulder and walked up the aisle between the banked seats. There was no sign of the girl.

"Fay?" Suzie called, peering into the shadows. She wondered where Fay had disappeared to.

Suzie was about to go and practise her skating when she heard a small voice call from behind the highest row of seats.

"Suzie—I'm here."

Suzie ran up the aisle, relieved that Fay was still here. "I couldn't find you. I thought you'd gone."

She came to a sudden halt on the top step, staring.

The girl was crouching behind a seat, curled into a ball and hugging her shins. Except … the girl was no longer Fay.

Suzie took a step backward, her heart hammering in her chest.

"Who are you?"

"I'm Fay of course. Please, don't be alarmed."

The girl rose to her feet and smiled, and Suzie almost fainted.

She remembered thinking yesterday that the girl had changed in the short time she had known her. Well, she had changed even more now. She was no longer a thin, pale girl. She was taller, and no longer skinny. Her clothing had changed, too: now she wore black leggings and an orange sweatshirt.…

But the greatest change was in the colour of her skin. Today the girl was black.

Suzie was staring at an exact copy of herself.

"Don't be frightened, Suzie. It really is me—Fay."

"How … how did you …?" Suzie stared. It was like looking into a mirror and seeing her reflection.

"We—my people—have the ability to change shape."

It came to Suzie, then, in a sudden, dizzying rush. "You…. That meteor—it *was* a spaceship!"

"I lost control on entry into Earth's atmosphere. Engine malfunction. I had to abandon ship before it hit the ground. I came down in a life capsule on the edge of town. In order to pass among your people, I changed shape into the first person I saw—a young girl."

Suzie shook her head, hardly able to believe what she was hearing. "But … but why change again—why change into me?"

"For protection. The people who run this place know you. This morning, when the rink opened, I went down and skated on the ice. No one asked who I was, what I was doing here. They thought I was you."

Suzie's legs felt weak and she sank to the ground. "I don't believe I'm really hearing this."

Fay sat down beside her. Suzie realized that they must look like twins, sitting there side by side.

"I come from a planet many light years from Earth," Fay said, "a planet called Vallaria, which orbits the star you know as Beta Hydri. My planet is cold, as cold as the Arctic here on Earth. To me, your country is too hot. The air burns my lungs. That is why I need the cold, the ice."

"But why have you come to Earth?" Suzie asked.

"To explore," the alien replied. "I intended to land in an uninhabited region of Earth, so that I would not be discovered. Then I could gather samples of rock and flora, and then report back to my people. We have been coming to your planet for many hundreds of your years."

"And you've never made yourself known to us?"

The alien smiled. It was a smile Suzie had seen many times before, in the mirror. "My people decided long ago that we should not contact your people. You are … you are still a young race. You are still angry and violent. We feared that you would be suspicious of our intentions, and try to find some way to harm us. In years to come, when you have grown as a race and dispensed with violence, then we will make ourselves known to you."

Suzie stared at the alien, trying to take in all that it had said. "If you can change shape at random," she said, "then what's your real shape? What do you look like normally?"

Fay shook her head. "You would find me … ugly, repulsive to look at. I am too *different*—"

"Then you're not really a girl, like me?"

The alien smiled again.

"On Vallaria we do not have males and females. We are all one sex. And I am not young. By the reckoning of my people I am middle-aged. But by your reckoning I am almost 100 years old."

Suzie opened her mouth in amazement. Fay said, "Later today a rescue ship will come for me and take me away from here. I want you to know that you saved my life—what is wrong?"

Suzie was staring down at the entrance of the rink.

Kim Reed and her friends were standing around, watching the people going to and from the ice. Kim had come here only once before on Saturday morning: she had waited for Suzie to finish her practice, and then found her and dragged her outside.…

Fay touched her arm. "Suzie, what is it?"

"They … those girls, down there."

"They are your enemies, Suzie? They are the people who bully?"

Suzie nodded, fearing that Kim would look up and see her.

Fay took her arm. "Get down. Hide behind the seat!"

Suzie ducked. "What are you going to do?"

"Stay there and do not move."

"Don't go near them, Fay. You don't know what they're like. They'll hurt you—"

Fay stared into Suzie's eyes. "You saved my life, Suzie. Now I will do something for you."

And before Suzie could protest, Fay set off and ran down the aisle toward Kim Reed and her friends.

Suzie peered over the back of the seat. Fay had said something to Kim and was walking slowly toward the exit. A second later Kim and the others gave chase. Suzie watched them leave the rink, a sick feeling in her stomach.

She recalled what Kim and her friends had done to her, the last time.… She closed her eyes. She would rather not remember what had happened, back then.

She decided that she could not let the alien suffer what she had suffered. She stood and ran down the aisle.

She hurried from the building, dazzled by the bright morning sunlight. She looked left and right, up and down the street, but there was no sign of the alien and Kim. Desperate, she turned left and dodged among the shoppers, then stopped. She realized that it was hopeless. She had no chance of finding them now. She would return to the rink, sit on the steps, and wait until Fay got back.

• • •

She waited for two hours, but the alien never turned up.

At midday she decided to go home. She would come back later, and with luck Fay would have returned safely.

She left the rink and walked across town. She was thinking about Fay's icy homeworld, Vallaria, when she heard someone calling her name.

She turned and saw Kim Reed walking toward her. Suzie froze, her stomach heaving in panic.

Kim stopped, towering above Suzie. She was looking down at Suzie, an odd expression on her face.

"I've been thinking about what you told me," Kim said quickly. She could hardly look Suzie in the eye, as if ashamed. "You're right. What we were doing—it was wrong. We shouldn't have got you, just because you're different...." She made an awkward gesture with her hands, obviously finding the apology difficult.

Suzie watched her without a word, wondering what the alien had said to Kim.

"Look," Kim went on, "anybody says they'll get you, just tell me. I'll make sure you're okay."

Kim smiled at her, then turned and hurried away.

• • •

Suzie was almost home when someone shouted "Suzie!" and she knew straight away who it was.

She turned. "Fay?"

The alien, still looking like a reflection of Suzie, stood at the corner of an alleyway, gesturing to her. She pulled Suzie between the buildings.

"I am leaving very soon. I wanted to say goodbye, and to thank you."

"And I want to thank you. What did you say to Kim? I saw her just now."

"I explained to her that what she was doing was wrong."

Suzie laughed. "And she listened to you—just like that?"

Fay smiled. "Of course not. I had to … persuade her. Shape-changing is not my only ability. I entered her mind and made her see that what she had been doing was wrong. I made her experience how she would feel if people victimized her because of *her* differences.…"

The alien reached out and took Suzie's hand. "It was the least I could do, in return for your help."

There was a sound from behind the alien. Suzie stared down the alley. From nowhere, filling what seconds earlier had been emptiness, a silver object like a cone appeared. A circular hole opened in the side of the thing, and a blast of icy air whistled out. Suzie hugged herself against the cold.

She looked back at Fay. The alien was changing shape before her very eyes. Fay's face altered, lost its black pigmentation. The orange sweatshirt slowly disappeared, along with the leggings.

The alien was turning green.

Suzie backed away. Fay—the alien—stood before her, more like an upright frog than a human, its slick green skin glistening in the sunlight.

The alien held out its hand. "Suzie, please do not be afraid. I am still me, after all. I am the creature you saved—only *different.*"

Overcoming her fear, telling herself that the alien's appearance did not matter, Suzie reached out and took its cold hand in hers.

"Thank you, Suzie," Fay said, then turned and walked toward the silver object.

Suzie watched as Fay stepped into the spaceship. The circular hatch closed behind her, became again the silver surface of the cone. Then, as suddenly as the spaceship had appeared, it was gone.

Suzie felt a sudden stab of sadness. She wanted to shout at Fay to come back, to talk to her. There was so much she wanted to tell the alien, so much she wanted to share with her friend.

She wondered when the aliens would show themselves again, how long it might be before they judged the human race civilized enough to contact.

She looked up, into the cloudless summer sky. She told herself that she could see a bright silver speck, flying high.

"Goodbye, Fay," Suzie N'Dah whispered, "and thank you."

Reflect on

Strategies: Find two places in the story where you made personal connections that will help with your retelling.

Your Learning: You know science fiction can make readers think about today's issues. What new ideas about today's issues do you have after reading this story?

SPACE TECHNOLOGY

In this unit, you will

- make inferences
- identify the text features of an activity
- analyze elements of writing fluency
- identify conventions and techniques used in toy packaging
- learn about technology used in space exploration

Quiz: From Space to Earth

smoke detector

firefighter suit

TV satellite dish

ear thermometer

Materials and technology developed for space exploration have led to the creation of many useful products right here on Earth. Which of the items shown below do you think have links to space research?

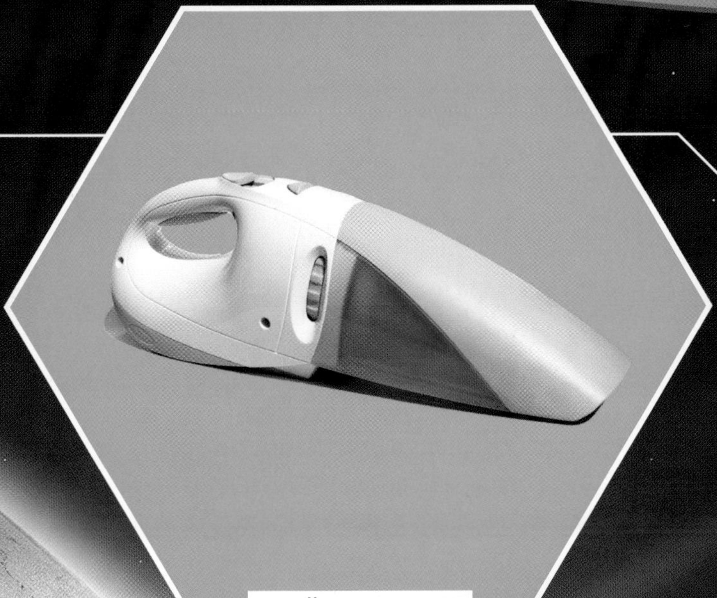

cordless vacuum

metal wires in braces

computer game joystick

sports safety helmet

Making Inferences

When you read, you use what you know and clues the author gives you to make inferences. Your inferences can help you draw conclusions and increase your understanding of what you are reading.

→

Ask yourself questions to uncover clues in the text. What can you infer about the authors' purpose by what they tell you and by their word choices?

At Home on the

INTERNATIONAL SPACE STATION

by the editors of *YES Mag*

Part 1

The International Space Station (ISS) is a giant laboratory where astronauts do experiments to learn more about space, and to make discoveries that will be useful on Earth. On the ISS, astronauts have to adapt to a very different way of life.

Meals That Are Out of This World

Barfing, sneezing, and sore backs (these are all effects of microgravity in space) eventually take a back seat to coping with everyday life on the ISS—the simple facts of eating and sleeping become adventures. Come on board and join the crew for a visit and a not-so-quick bite to eat. Most days, the ISS astronauts have 90 minutes to prepare and eat a meal. Here's how food prep happens.

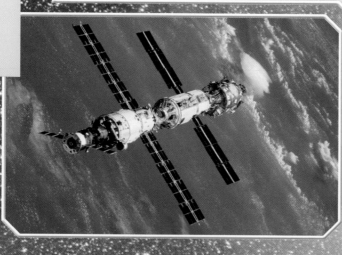

Astronauts may live on the ISS for up to six months.

Astronauts on the ISS share a meal.

You go to Zvezda Service Module, where the galley is located, and grab a meal tray. You choose a meal listed on the computer. (The meals are selected five months before liftoff. Astronauts must decide then what they want to eat for their entire stay on the ISS.) Menus have been analyzed for nutritional content. One nutrient of concern during long stints in space is vitamin D, which is important for bone health. The lack of ultraviolet light from the Sun, due to spacecraft shielding, limits the ability of astronauts' bodies to produce this vitamin naturally.

But back to the computer. You type in "chicken teriyaki with stir-fried vegetables." The computer tells you which drawer to find your meal in. You put the packaged meal into a convection oven. While the chicken and veggies are heating, you rehydrate some wonton soup by plugging in a needle-shaped water faucet and pressing the hot water button. To stop fluid from escaping, you slurp the soup through a straw that has a clip at the end.

← Use your personal experiences and background knowledge. What can you infer about the size of the team and the planning that goes into an ISS mission?

Astronaut Brian Duffy tests a space drink at NASA's Johnson Space Center.

Astronauts join in a toast by "clinking" bags of juice.

When the chicken and veggies are cooked, you take the package out of the oven and Velcro it to the tray. Then you strap the tray to a table and start to eat. Take it slowly—no sudden movements. Knocking over your meal would mean floating chicken and veggies. Small squeeze bottles—sort of like eye-drop bottles—containing salt water and pepper water let you season your food. For dessert, there's a fortune cookie. Your fortune: You have the ability to rise above others.

Combine your knowledge and your inferences to draw conclusions. What are some personal qualities an astronaut would need to be happy in space?

Flying Food

Food is delivered to the ISS by the space shuttle or the Russian Progress supply vehicles about once a month. A delivery means fresh fruit and veggies. Most food is made to last—it's dehydrated, frozen, or processed, and packaged in pouches and cans. The packaging is ultra important. It must withstand pressures rarely exerted by your average grocery store clerk: the cans experience the same jarring forces the astronauts feel during takeoff.

Space food must also be germ free—no one wants sick astronauts. On Earth, the acceptable amount of bacteria for canned food is about 300 000 bacteria per gram. In space, it's a minuscule 8 bacteria per gram. Food must also be solid—sauce floating around is not only messy, it's germ friendly.

Packaging the parts of a meal in plastic bags helps keep things neat and organized on the ISS.

At Home on the INTERNATIONAL SPACE STATION

47

Applying Strategies

Making Inferences

As you read this article, make inferences and draw conclusions to increase your understanding of what you are reading:

- Ask yourself questions to uncover clues in the text.
- Use your personal experiences and background knowledge.
- Combine your knowledge and your inferences to draw conclusions.

Part 2

Clean Up!

There are no fights over dirty dishes on the International Space Station—everything is chucked into the trash compactor. But there is other cleaning to do, and for that there's nothing like good old-fashioned elbow grease. The ISS crew keeps surfaces clean by—are you ready for this?— wiping them down with a mild soap.

All surfaces are cleaned about every two weeks, more often when food is spilled. Not only do astronauts make a mess, they are the mess. Astronauts lose up to 3 g of skin daily. This dead skin, lint, plus all of the other stuff that makes up dust, free floats around in the station. The debris eventually finds its way to air filters, which also pick up tiny hitchhikers called micro-organisms.

Astronauts bring micro-organisms—fungi and bacteria—with them into space and liberally sprinkle them around the station. People-eating aliens from interstellar space pale in comparison to what these renegade life-forms could do. With no natural competitors in space, colonies of micro-organisms could choke out any other life.

Cosmonaut Mikhail Tyurin gives astronaut Frank Culbertson a haircut. Frank uses a modified vacuum to suck up the clippings.

Air filters get rid of the dust and micro-organisms, then the filters are vacuumed to keep them clean. But one other hitchhiker, mold, is immune to all that vacuuming and filtering. Mold, which is a type of fungus, especially loves humidity and will eat just about anything. Fungus was actually eating through the glass portholes of the Russian space station *Mir*. To discourage mold, the ISS is kept dry. Its humidity levels are set at 65 to 70 percent. Unfortunately, that means more flaky skin—and more cleaning!

Canadian astronaut Chris Hadfield makes sure a window is sparkling clean.

Ship's Log:
Dec. 11, 2000

Went through the ship with the vacuum cleaner—pulled all the debris out of filters and intakes. It is amazing—if you ever let go of something, there is an almost 100 percent chance it is going to end up in a filter or screen somewhere.

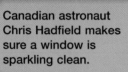

Breathe Easy

Imagine sharing a cramped space for months without showers or even a window that opens. Whew!

Relax—you can breathe easy on the ISS. It's equipped with machines that scrub the air and provide fresh oxygen. While some oxygen is stored, the ISS can use electricity from its solar panels to create oxygen from water.

Great! Now you've got oxygen to breathe in, but what about the carbon dioxide you breathe out? Some of it is vented into space. The rest is combined with hydrogen to produce water and a gas called methane. The water is re-used, and the methane is released into space.

Good Night

You've worked for at least eight hours. Exercised for two. Spent a lot of time preparing your meals. Contacted friends and family by e-mail. Watched a Russian movie with subtitles, and now you're pretty tired.

On the ISS, astronauts store their personal stuff, look for quiet time, and sleep in a "bedroom" smaller than your average bunk bed. But at least they have somewhere quiet to go. Actually, it's not all that quiet. The rattle of fans and machinery force the crew to wear earplugs when they sleep.

When it's time to catch some *zzzzs*, astronauts pull off their slipper-socks and outer clothing, storing everything in a net. They climb into their sleeping bags and pull up the long zipper on the front of the bag, then snap together straps around their waists to hold them securely in their bunks. One warning: in the microgravity of the space station, arms float out in front like Frankenstein's monster's. To keep that from happening, astronauts slip their hands through loops on the side of the sleeping bag.

Sleep is scheduled for eight hours, but often astronauts wake frequently, especially during longer space missions. Scientists believe that in space the body's internal clock is disrupted. This clock regulates the body's daily production of hormones that help you sleep and feel awake. The clock is reset every day by the rising and setting sun. But on the station, one "day" is just 90 minutes long—bright half the time, dark the other half. So while some astronauts take sleeping pills, on average, astronauts still sleep two hours less each night than on Earth.

Cosmonaut Yury Usachev jots down some notes in his cozy sleeping compartment.

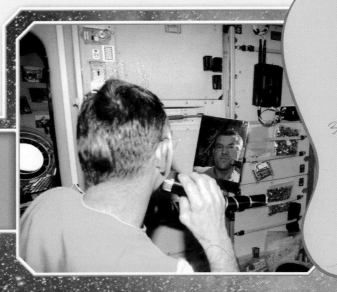

After a good night's sleep, astronaut James Voss shaves to get ready for a new day on the ISS.

Reflect on

Strategies: How did making inferences and drawing conclusions help you to increase your understanding of space technology?

Critical Literacy: How would you describe the authors' point of view on the International Space Station? Do you think they were trying to influence your point of view? Why?

Text Features of an Activity

Books, magazines, and web pages often contain hands-on activities to help you understand new concepts. Activities have certain text features:

- An activity has a title and brief introduction.
- Headings tell what kinds of information you are given.
- Photos or illustrations give you information.

SUIT UP FOR SPACE

by Kevin Choy

Part 1

Explorers need to dress appropriately for the environment. Heading off on a scientific expedition to the South Pole? You'll need a thick parka and long underwear. Trekking through the Sahara? Be sure to pack sunglasses and a sun hat.

Now imagine that you're planning to do a spacewalk in outer space, a place where temperatures in direct sunlight can reach 120 °C. Move into the shade, and the temperature drops to a bone-chilling −100 °C or even lower. Temperature isn't the only challenge of the outer space environment. There is almost no oxygen, so you'd be unconscious in 15 seconds. The lack of air pressure would make your body fluids bubble up, causing your skin and internal organs to expand (ouch!). No doubt about it, you've got to dress right for space!

To protect yourself on a spacewalk, you'll need a spacesuit—an Extravehicular Mobility Unit (EMU). It has everything you need to stay alive and safe. The body of the suit is made from many layers of high-tech materials, protecting you from heat, cold, and even dangers such as micrometeoroids. (A puncture in your space suit would be deadly.)

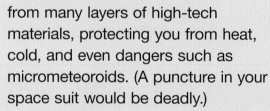

Astronaut Phillippe Perrin wears his spacesuit as he helps with construction on the International Space Station.

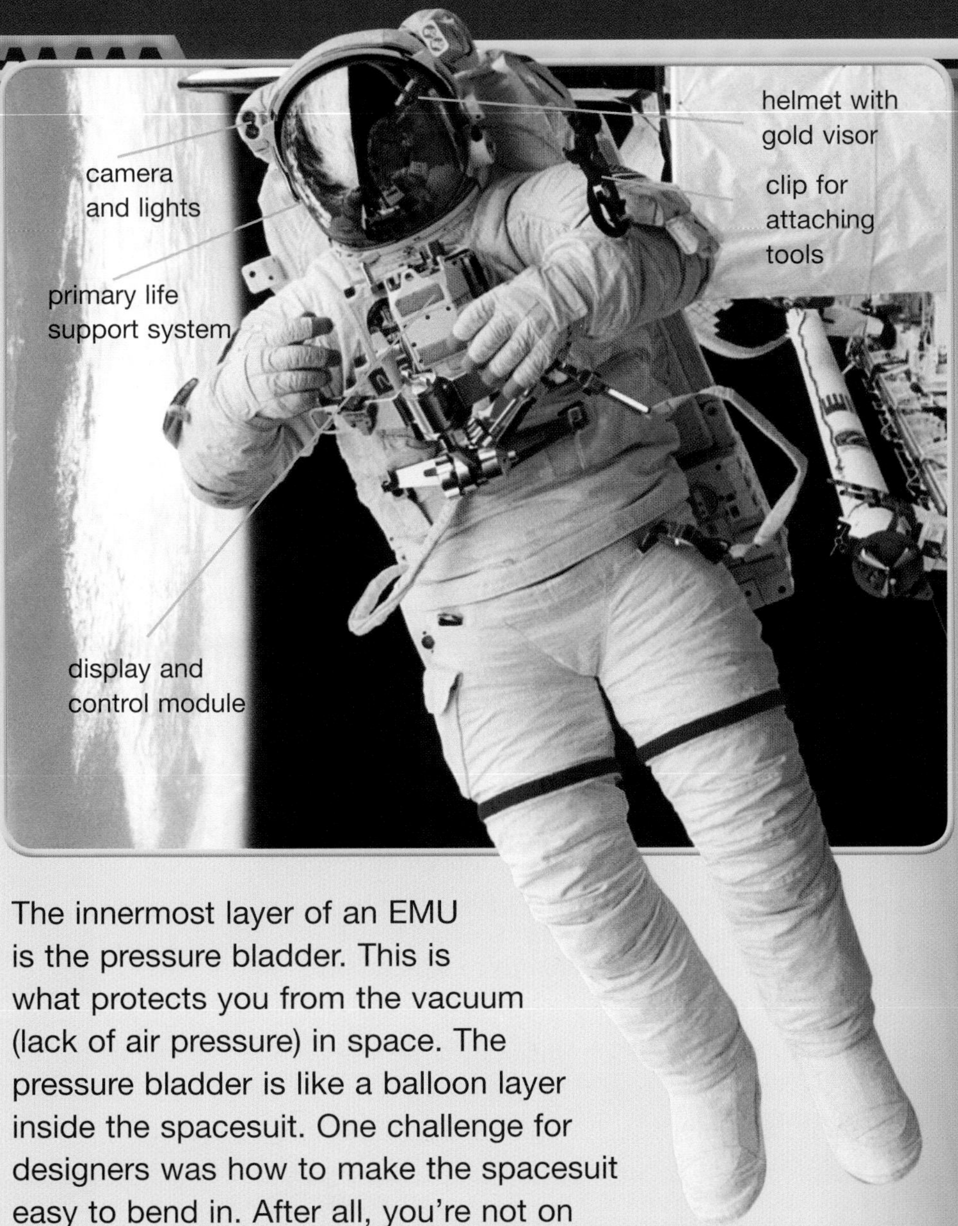

camera
and lights

primary life
support system

display and
control module

helmet with
gold visor

clip for
attaching
tools

The innermost layer of an EMU
is the pressure bladder. This is
what protects you from the vacuum
(lack of air pressure) in space. The
pressure bladder is like a balloon layer
inside the spacesuit. One challenge for
designers was how to make the spacesuit
easy to bend in. After all, you're not on
a spacewalk just for the fun of it. You have important tasks
to complete and you need to be able to bend your arms and
legs. The pressure bladder can make bending difficult, but your
spacesuit has been designed to overcome this. The pressure
bladder has special "joints," or breaking points, that make it
easier for you to bend.

An activity has a title and brief introduction. How do the title and introduction help you to understand the purpose of this activity? →

Headings tell what kind of information you are given. What information are you given in this activity? →

Photos or illustrations give you information. What do you learn from the photos in this activity?

Activity: Balloon Spacesuits

Adapted from the Canadian Space Agency website

Try this activity to understand why spacesuits have "joints" or breaking points to make it easier for astronauts to bend their arms and legs.

What you need:

- 2 long balloons
- 3 heavy-duty rubber bands

What you do:

1. Blow up and tie off one long balloon. This balloon represents the pressure bladder of a spacesuit arm.

2. Start blowing up the second balloon. As you do this, have a partner slip the rubber bands around the balloon at intervals. The balloon should be pinched by the rubber bands in three different places. Then tie off the balloon. The rubber bands represent the "joints" in a spacesuit's pressure bladder.

3. Try to bend the balloon without the rubber bands. Then try to bend the balloon with the rubber bands. Which balloon takes more force to bend?

Think About It

What would be the difference between wearing a spacesuit with and without "joints" or breaking points? How might a spacesuit without "joints" affect an astronaut doing a long and difficult repair?

SUIT UP FOR SPACE

Applying Strategies

Text Features of an Activity

As you read, remember to look for these text features of an activity:

- An activity has a title and brief introduction.
- Headings tell what kind of information you are given.
- Photos or illustrations give you information.

Part 2

The 14 layers of a spacesuit will help to keep you warm when you're out of the sun. But how will you stay cool when the temperature starts to rise? That's the job of the Liquid Cooling and Ventilation Garment. Think of it as long underwear with tubing running through it. The tubes carry cool liquids all over your body to keep you at a comfortable temperature.

Other important components of your spacesuit include

- **Primary Life Support System (PLSS):** Along with providing oxygen, the PLSS backpack has many other important functions, such as providing power and transmitting information back to Mission Control.

- **Displays and Control Module (DCM):** Worn on the chest, this box controls the PLSS as well as the secondary oxygen pack you carry along, just in case. One switch controls a ventilation fan that circulates air through your helmet and other parts of the suit. A "push-to-talk" switch lets you communicate with fellow astronauts or with Mission Control. There are many other controls on the DCM, including one that lets you adjust the pressure inside the suit.

- **Helmet:** A valve in your helmet releases the carbon dioxide you breathe out. When you need to work in the sun, you add a special attachment with a gold visor. This visor is the spacesuit version of sunglasses. Attached to each side of your helmet are lights and a camera.

All in all, there are 18 different parts to your spacesuit, giving it a total weight of 114 kg. You'll need some help, and about 45 minutes, to get into it. A spacesuit may not be the height of fashion, but at a cost of about $12 million, it's more expensive than any designer outfit!

Astronaut Heidemarie Stefanyshyn-Piper trains for a spacewalk by practising wearing her spacesuit underwater.

Activity: Spacesuits and Heat

Adapted from the Canadian Space Agency website

Try this activity to understand why spacesuits need to keep astronauts cool.

What you need:

- a kitchen-size plastic garbage bag
- tape

What you do:

1. If you're wearing long sleeves, roll up one sleeve.

2. Wrap the plastic bag around your bare arm, but not too tightly. Have a partner use a couple of pieces of tape to keep the bag from unwrapping.

3. Wave your covered arm around for two minutes.

4. Remove the bag and notice how your arm feels.

Think About It

Did your arm feel cooler once you removed the bag? Why do you think this happens? What does this tell you about spacesuits?

Activity: Staying Cool in Space

Adapted from the Canadian Space Agency website

Try this activity to understand how spacesuits keep astronauts cool.

What you need:

- 2 buckets
- 3 m of new aquarium tubing
- enough ice to fill half of one bucket
- clean tap water

What you do:

1. Thoroughly wash and rinse one bucket and put it on a desk. Add the ice and then fill the bucket with water.

2. Carefully wash and rinse one end of the tubing.

3. Sit on a chair in front of the desk, with the empty bucket on the floor beside you.

4. Have a partner wrap the tubing (snugly but not too tightly) around your bare arm, as shown in the photo. The washed end of the tubing should extend down from your hand.

5. Ask your partner to put one end (not the washed end) of the tubing in the ice water.

6. Have your partner suck on the washed end of the tubing just until the water starts to flow over your partner's shoulder. Quickly place this end of the tubing in the empty bucket. (Do not share tubing that has been in someone's mouth.)

7. Notice how your arm feels as the water flows through the tubing.

Think About It

In what occupations here on Earth would a suit with a cooling system be useful?

Reflect on

Strategies: How might knowing the characteristics of an activity format be helpful to someone doing the activity?

Connections: What kinds of resources do you think a country would need to participate in space exploration?

Blast Off for Fun

Conventions and Techniques in Toy Packaging

Media texts use conventions and techniques (ways of creating an effect) to make the audience react in a certain way. How do the designers of toy packaging want you to react? They hope you'll feel excited by the text and want to buy the toy!

What conventions and techniques do you find on toy packages? The words and images are carefully chosen, and lots of attention is paid to how these are arranged on the package.

Every centimetre of the box surface is used. How many messages in words and pictures can you identify? Why do you think the box is so "busy" looking?

Includes CD guided audio tour of the night sky!

Transforms a darkened room into a 360° space theater!

Includes interactive Meteor Maker™

STAR THEATER 2

HOME PLANETARIUM with interactive Meteor Maker™

uncle Milton

2002
AGES 8 AND UP

Words on the box are carefully chosen. Why do you think the word "includes" appears twice on the box? What feelings do the words "transforms" and "interactive" give you?

The quality of the design and the images used on the package are part of the message. What do you think the toy maker wants you to infer about this toy?

Evaluate the packaging on this page. What conventions and techniques did the designer use? How would you rate the effectiveness of this package?

Analyzing Elements of Fluency

Good writers make their writing "fluent," meaning that sentences and paragraphs flow naturally from one to the next and offer variety to keep readers interested. By analyzing the work of other writers, you can learn how to build fluency into your own writing.

Look for elements of fluency as you read this short article. Notice how the writer varies sentence beginnings and sentence lengths, and uses transitions and punctuation to create flow.

ANOUSHEH ANSARI
АНЮШЕ АНСАРИ

Space Tourists

Got $20 million? It will cost you at least that much to become a space tourist. Forget about making last-minute plans—first you'll need about six months of training. Learning how to walk and breathe in a spacesuit are just two of the things you'll have to work on.

In April 2001, Dennis Tito, an entrepreneur and former NASA scientist, became the first space tourist when he spent a week on the International Space Station (ISS). At the time, NASA and the space agencies of Canada, Europe, and Japan said Tito's trip was a one-time exception. It wasn't.

The fourth space tourist, tech businesswoman Anousheh Ansari, went into the record books with her 2006 flight; she was the first female space tourist. Software engineer Charles Simonyi became the fifth tourist when he flew to the ISS on a Russian spacecraft in 2007. He won't be the last. The world's largest space agencies have now developed health and training standards for space tourists.

How to analyze elements of fluency:

✔ Find a piece of writing you think is very good and read it several times.

✔ Look for variety in the sentence beginnings.

✔ Count the words in each sentence, and decide if there is variety in sentence lengths.

✔ Identify the transitions, and figure out how transitions provide links between sentences and paragraphs.

✔ Notice the punctuation, especially punctuation within sentences. Ask yourself, "How do commas, semicolons, colons, and dashes create fluency?"

EXPLORING MARS

by Barbara Hehner

Applying Strategies

Reading Like a Writer

As you read this article, analyze the elements of fluency. Notice variety in sentence beginnings and sentence lengths. Figure out how transitions and punctuation create flow.

Mars Watchers

For hundreds of years, human beings have dreamed of travelling to Mars and exploring its mysteries. In the 1700s, astronomers began to focus their telescopes on Mars. In the 1800s, as telescopes became more and more powerful, scientists mapped some of Mars' biggest landforms, and first noted its two moons. But more detailed and accurate knowledge of the planet had to wait for the technology of the modern Space Age.

Fly-bys and Landers

As far back as the 1960s, three American spacecrafts, NASA's *Mariners 4, 6,* and *7,* flew past Mars, taking photographs of 20 percent of its surface. From these missions, scientists discovered that the south polar ice cap was made of frozen carbon dioxide, not frozen water. Since water has been essential for life on our own planet, the dream of finding microscopic forms of life on Mars had received a setback.

On December 2, 1971, the Soviet Union beat the United States in the race to place a lander on Mars. (Landers were designed to stay in one spot and transmit data back to Earth.) However, the lander's instruments stopped working after just 20 seconds, probably because of a huge Martian dust storm that was raging at the time.

Both countries had several failed Mars missions during the 1970s, but the United States finally had a double success with the orbiters and landers of *Viking 1* and *Viking 2. Viking 1* was launched in August 1975 and its lander touched down on Mars on June 20, 1976. *Viking 2* was launched in September of 1975 and the lander touched down on September 3, 1976. The orbiters circled the planet, sending back photographs of its entire surface. For the first time, people on Earth had a detailed look at Martian volcanos and lava plains, canyons and craters.

Thanks to modern technology, we have much clearer views of Mars than ever before. This photo was taken by the Hubble Telescope.

Meanwhile, the landers transmitted close-up shots of the planet's gritty surface, while their instruments onboard studied the Martian soil. Were there organic compounds—the building blocks of living things—which might point to life on Mars? At first it seemed there might be, but most scientists finally decided that the soil did not contain organic compounds. It would be twenty years before a spacecraft returned to Mars to take another look.

Mars Sojourner rover

Roving on Mars

Launched on December 4, 1996, the U.S. Pathfinder mission arrived on a rocky Martian plain on July 4, 1997. There, its lander spacecraft rolled out something new: a rover called Sojourner. Sojourner was a six-wheeled vehicle about the size of a child's wagon, weighing 10.6 kg. Sojourner could travel about 500 m from the lander, controlled by scientists back on Earth.

In its three months of operation, Sojourner took photographs, analyzed some interesting rocks in its path, and sent back millions of measurements of the Martian climate. It was a thrilling achievement, but even better was to come.

Spirit and Opportunity

On June 10 and July 7, 2003, NASA launched twin spacecrafts toward Mars, carrying identical rovers called Spirit and Opportunity. Spirit's spacecraft arrived first, on January 4, 2004. As it neared Mars, the lander opened its parachute, which slowed its descent. Its retrorockets fired 12 times, slowing it down even more. Just before the lander hit the Martian surface, its 24 airbags deployed, looking like a bunch of grapes that cushioned the lander on all sides. It rolled and bounced a dozen times before coming to a stop at its landing site, the Gusev Crater. Finally, the doors opened, and the Spirit rover rolled outside. The first thing Spirit did was to transmit a 360-degree picture of its surroundings back to Earth.

Landing Spirit and Opportunity

1. The lander's parachute and retrorockets bring the lander to a halt 10 m above the surface of Mars. The protective airbags inflate.

2. After being released from the parachute, the lander bounces and rolls before coming to a stop.

3. The lander opens and the rover drives onto the Martian surface.

Opportunity landed safely on January 25, 2004. Its landing site was the Meridiani Planum, a plain on the other side of Mars from the Gusev Crater.

The two rovers were well equipped for scientific exploring. Their onboard computers each had 1000 times more memory than Sojourner's. The rovers were also much larger and sturdier than Sojourner—each one about the size of a golf cart. They had wide, flat tops covered with solar panels to power their batteries during the Martian day. The rovers' tops were equipped with cameras mounted on a mast, as well as magnets to attract Martian dust that could then be analyzed.

Each rover had a robotic arm attached to the front. Like a human arm, it could move at the shoulder, elbow, and wrist. At the end of the arm was a device holding four tools. This device could turn to install the right tool for the right job on the arm's "wrist." The various tools could provide close-up images of rocks and soil, analyze what they were made of, and grind away the weathered surface of rocks to expose fresh material underneath. No wonder NASA scientists called the rovers the "robot geologists"!

Armed with these tools, the rovers were to explore the mission's biggest question: had water activity on Mars affected the planet's environment? Although there is no liquid water on Mars now, the marks of water in the past might be found in land formations, rocks, and soil. While looking for evidence of water, the mission had four scientific goals:

1. Determine whether life ever arose on Mars

2. Describe the climate of Mars

3. Describe the geology of Mars

4. Prepare for human exploration

This is an artist's image of one of the Mars rovers at work.

One of Spirit's wheels uncovered light material in the Martian soil. This material is silica, which on Earth is found in soil once covered by water. The presence of silica is strong evidence that water once existed in the Gusev Crater.

Mission Accomplished?

So how well have the rovers done?

Goal 1: They did not find any living organisms, but they found ample evidence that Mars once had lots of water. Water may have made it possible for tiny life forms, such as bacteria, to evolve on the planet.

Goal 2: For several years, both rovers have provided daily weather reports from Mars. Scientists are still not agreed on whether the evidence points to a planet that was once warmer or colder than it is now.

Goal 3: The rovers have found and analyzed many rock and soil samples, concentrating on minerals that contain iron. Iron-bearing minerals are associated with the presence of water.

Goal 4: The rovers' mission was supposed to last 90 days. But after three years they were still carrying out scientific investigations. This shows that human beings who travel to Mars can be equipped with tools tough enough to withstand the dust storms and temperature extremes of Mars for a long period.

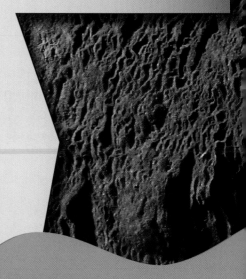

In August 2007, Opportunity and Spirit were facing their greatest challenge—severe dust storms that lasted for weeks and kept sunlight away from their solar panels. NASA scientists kept the rovers powered down to try to ride out the storms.

Meanwhile, NASA launched a new lander, scheduled to reach the Martian North Pole in May 2008 to investigate the ice there.

Plans are already underway for an even more ambitious rover. Twice as long and three times as heavy as Spirit and Opportunity, the Mars Science Laboratory will collect Martian soil and rock samples and analyze them for organic compounds. This mission will have international support, with instruments provided by both the Canadian and Russian Space Agencies.

Before the middle of the twenty-first century, if all goes as planned, human space explorers will set foot on Mars for the first time. It is likely that their journey and arrival will bring new challenges and surprises. But they will not be entering an unknown world. Thanks to developments in space technology, we have already learned a great deal about Mars since people first peered through telescopes at this intriguing planet.

Reflect on

Writer's Craft: Find three places in the article where you can explain how the writer created fluency.

Your Learning: What did you learn in this article that will help you to follow the unfolding story of Mars exploration in the decades ahead?

A HELPING HAND IN SPACE

by Valerie Wyatt

Next time you're outdoors on a cloudless night, keep an eye out for the International Space Station (ISS) passing overhead. Orbiting about 325 km above you, it is one of the brightest human-made objects in the sky. From Earth it looks like a slow-moving star.

Inside that dot of light, three astronauts live and work. Their only protection from the hostile environment of space is the thin skin of the ISS. If something goes wrong with the space station's exterior, the astronauts know what to do. They climb into their spacesuits and go for an EVA—Extravehicular Activity. Translation: they go for a spacewalk and fix it.

Spacewalks are risky for astronauts. Even something as minor as a torn glove can turn into a major problem—a tear can threaten an astronaut's oxygen supply. Up to now, astronauts on the ISS have had a helper to keep EVAs short and safe—Canadarm2, a made-in-Canada robotic arm.

The first Canadarm, attached to a space shuttle, was sent into space in 1981. Then Canadarm2, launched in 2001, helped build the ISS and has been used to repair and maintain it ever since. An astronaut inside the ISS uses a computer to control Canadarm2, while astronauts outside work alongside it to make repairs or do other jobs, such as unloading cargo or moving scientific equipment.

Attached to the ISS, Canadarm2 has three joints, similar to a human shoulder, elbow, and wrist.

Canadarm2 works like your arm. It has joints in three places (like your shoulder, elbow, and wrist) and a snare-like hand that can grasp things. But there is one big difference between your arm and the Canadarm: it is 15 m long and strong enough to lift a busload of people.

As of 2008, there'll be a new helper in space. It's the Special Purpose Dexterous Manipulator, or Dextre for short. It has been designed by the same team who built Canadarm2 and uses some of the same technology, but Dextre is far more dexterous than the Canadarm.

The new kid in space looks a bit like a robot with no head and two 3.5 m long arms. Its body can turn at the waist and shoulders, and each of its arms has seven joints, giving it greater flexibility than the Canadarm.

At the end of Dextre's arms are "hands," officially known as Orbital Replacement Unit/Tool Changeout Mechanisms, or OTCMs. These hands can grasp objects or tools—whatever is needed to get the job done. Four built-in cameras and lights mounted on Dextre give astronauts inside the ISS a good view of the work area as they control the space robot from the safety of the space station.

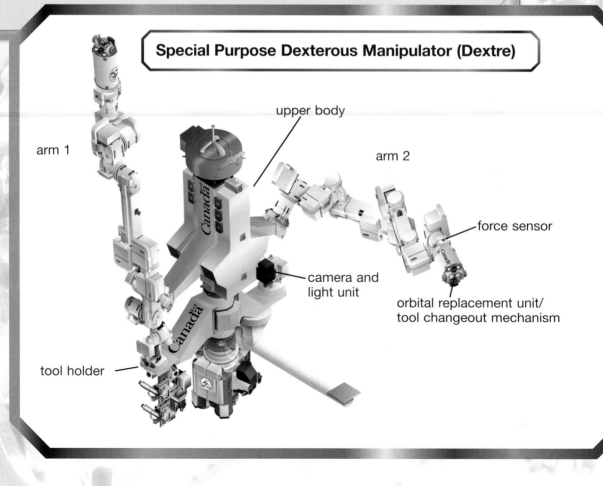

Special Purpose Dexterous Manipulator (Dextre)

arm 1

upper body

arm 2

force sensor

camera and light unit

orbital replacement unit/ tool changeout mechanism

tool holder

Dextre is strong enough to move heavy cargo, but it's also gentle. Its touch is so delicate that it can perform tasks such as loosening bolts and replacing batteries in tight spaces. Dextre's makers equipped the robot with special sensors that act somewhat like the touch sensors in your hands. Its sensors can feel movement and make adjustments as it works. The astronauts give Dextre the basic instructions, and the touch sensors take care of the details.

Learning to operate Dextre requires hours and hours of training. Long before Dextre's launch into space, astronauts began practising how to use it—in a swimming pool. Why do it in a pool? Working underwater provides a low gravity experience that is as close as you can get to conditions in space.

Since the real Dextre was still under construction in Brampton, Ontario, astronauts were training on a mock-up. Later, astronauts flew to Canada to do even more training on the real thing. Still more training and testing will be done at the Kennedy Space Center in Florida, where Dextre will be launched into space aboard a space shuttle.

The training, and the design of Dextre itself, is all about safety. Dextre was built to reduce the number of EVAs for astronauts on the ISS. The less time the crew spends outside, the less chance there is for accidents and problems. And by reducing the time needed for EVAs, Dextre will leave astronauts more time for scientific work.

You can follow Dextre's progress, starting in 2008, by entering "Dextre, ISS" in a search engine. And don't forget to search the skies for the International Space Station next time there's a clear, starry night.

Astronauts practise underwater as they learn how to use Dextre.

This artist's image shows Dextre attached to the end of Canadarm2.

Robot Arm Challenge

Adapted from the NASA website

To interact with their environment, robots often use arms with gripping devices attached at the ends. In this activity, you'll build a robot arm and then make gripping devices for it.

What you need:

- 4 wooden craft sticks with pre-drilled holes (available at craft and dollar stores
- 4 small brass paper fasteners
- 1 pencil
- assorted materials available at home or in the classroom

What you do:

1. Use brass fasteners to assemble the arms as shown in the photo.

2. Test your robot arm to make sure it works. When you open and close one end, the other end should open and close.

3. Try to pick up a pencil using the robot arm. What makes this difficult to do?

4. Using materials you find at home or in the classroom, make two gripping devices and attach them to the ends of your robot arm. Can your robot arm pick up the pencil? What other objects can it pick up?

Think About It

What kind of gripping devices could you create that could pick up soil and rock samples from a planet? Should each of the two grips be the same, or should they be different? You can test your ideas by trying to pick up sand or tiny pebbles.

Robot arm without gripping devices

Reflect on

Strategies: How did making inferences help you to draw conclusions? What elements of fluency in the article have you used in your own writing?

Connections: Why do you think Canadarm has become a modern-day symbol of Canada?

YOU in the WORLD

In this unit, you will

- evaluate the validity of texts

- identify characteristics of problem-and-solution-text pattern

- analyze points of view in media texts

- build on different points of view in discussions

- learn about taking action

- distinguish between revising and editing

Getting Involved

finding cures for diseases

providing recreational activities for children with disabilities

ending poverty

Do you want to make the world a better place? If you could get involved with just one of the causes shown below, which one would you choose? Why?

protecting rainforests

protecting endangered species

helping victims of natural disasters

Evaluating

You see print all around you—from books to magazines, from the web to newspapers. One of your jobs as a reader is to evaluate text. When you evaluate text, you draw conclusions about the validity, or trustworthiness, of the ideas and information.

$\rightarrow\uparrow$

Look for evidence that the writer has carefully researched the topic. What specific details on this page show you the writer researched her topic?

Ryan's Well

Part 1

by Kathy Cook

Six-year-old Ryan Hreljac sat in shock as he listened to his Grade 1 teacher, Nancy Prest, at Holy Cross Catholic School in Kemptville, Ontario. Launching a school-wide campaign, she spoke that day of the sad plight of children living in impoverished, disease-stricken parts of Africa, where there was little access to medicine, food, or clean water. Ryan winced when he heard that hundreds of thousands of African children die each year just from drinking contaminated water.

It was January 1998, and Holy Cross was raising money for African relief. "Every penny helps," Nancy Prest told her class. She explained that a single penny would buy a pencil; 25¢ would buy 175 vitamins; 60¢ would buy a two-month supply of medicine for one child; "and $70 pays for a well."

When Ryan's parents, Susan and Mark, got home later that day, Ryan rushed past his babysitter to greet them. "Mom, Dad, I need $70 for a well in Africa!" he said excitedly.

"That's nice, Ryan," his mother replied distractedly as his younger brother, Keegan, clung to her.

Over dinner, Ryan tried again.

"Ryan, $70 is a lot of money," his mother said.

The next evening Ryan brought the subject up again. "You don't understand," he said, tears filling his eyes. "Children are dying because they don't have clean water!"

Ryan Hreljac at age 6

Ryan (top row, fourth from left) is shown with his Grade 1 class at Holy Cross Catholic School.

Susan sat Ryan down. "If you're really serious about raising $70, you can do extra chores around the house," she said, assuming he would quickly forget his project.

Ryan's face lit up. To encourage him, Susan drew a red thermometer with 35 lines across it, each line representing $2. For every $2, Ryan could fill in a line and put his earnings into an old cookie tin. "But Ryan," Susan said, "you'll have to do *extra* chores, not just the ones you already do."

"Okay," he said.

His first job was to vacuum the house. While Keegan and Ryan's older brother, Jordan, played outside, Ryan cleaned for two hours. He got $2. A few days later, instead of watching a movie with the family, he washed windows. Another $2.

After hearing about Ryan's goal, Ryan's grandfather hired the three brothers to pick up pine cones for craft projects. When Ryan brought his spring report card home, his parents gave him a $5 reward for good grades. That, too, went into the tin.

By Easter, when the school's fundraising campaign ended, Ryan's class had raised nearly $30 in pennies.

"I'm still collecting for the well," Ryan told his teacher. Chore by chore, loonie by loonie, he had by now amassed $35.

Determine if the writer presents a clear point of view that matches the facts. What do you think is the writer's point of view on Ryan's story? How do the facts match this point of view?

→

Look for names of established organizations and public figures. What established organizations connect to Ryan's story?

As Susan left for work one morning, she glanced at the thermometer on the fridge. It was two thirds full. *Who do you give $70 to if you want to build a well in Africa?* she wondered. She called the school, but they didn't know. Then Brenda Cameron Couch, a friend who worked at an international development organization, told her of WaterCan, a small non-profit agency in Ottawa that funds and monitors well building in developing countries.

Brenda called WaterCan and told them about Ryan. "Seventy dollars might not be a lot, but this kid has worked hard for it," she said. "I'd like him to give you his money in person."

On the day of the meeting in late April, Ryan nervously handed his cookie tin to Nicole Bosley, WaterCan's executive director at the time. "There's an extra $5 here," he said, lowering his voice. "You might want to buy some hot lunches for the people making the well."

Ryan's family, left to right: older brother Jordan, father Mark, Ryan, mother Susan, younger brother Keegan

"Thank you, Ryan," Nicole said, smiling. She began telling him about WaterCan's clean-water projects, explaining that while $70 would buy a hand pump, it actually cost closer to $2000 to drill a well. Too young to appreciate such a large sum, Ryan replied, "I'll just do more chores, then."

The Canadian International Development Agency (CIDA) matches WaterCan's funds two for one, so Ryan would have to find almost $700 to build his well. That night Susan and Mark sat in bed discussing what to do. "He's come so far," Mark said. "We can't just tell him, 'Ryan, you tried, but you can't really make a difference.'" Yet how could a 6-year-old raise $700 just by doing chores?

The following week Brenda sent out an e-mail to family and friends telling them about Ryan's project. The next day her cousin, Blaine Cameron, e-mailed back. Touched by Ryan's actions, he wanted to send in a donation matching Ryan's. A few months later, *The Kemptville Advance*, a local newspaper, ran a story about Ryan, calling it "Making a Difference: Ryan's Well."

Summer came and Ryan, now 7, turned his attention from school to fun. Yet throughout the holidays he kept doing extra chores. Periodically, Susan forwarded his donations to WaterCan.

In early August Susan bumped into Derek Puddicombe, an old acquaintance and freelance journalist. When Susan told him about Ryan's efforts, Derek's interest was tweaked. "What a fantastic story! I bet the *Citizen* would buy it."

Derek interviewed Ryan and the *Ottawa Citizen* sent a photographer to take pictures. Every morning Ryan expectantly looked through the newspaper, but weeks passed and the story didn't show up. "Maybe they lost it," he said, disappointment on his face.

• • •

Meanwhile, WaterCan called to say that donations for Ryan's Well had passed $700. Ryan and Susan were invited to a September board meeting to hear Gizaw Shibru, director for Uganda at Canadian Physicians for Aid and Relief (CPAR). WaterCan funded well construction by giving money to CPAR-Uganda, which then partnered with local villagers and actually dug and maintained the wells.

When Gizaw arrived, he gave Ryan a warm hug. "I understand you got us a well," he said. "Thank you."

Gizaw had a list of locations in need of a well. With only 46 percent of Ugandans having access to safe water, the list was long. Ryan asked Gizaw if his well could be near a school. Gizaw scanned his notes and told Ryan that it could be built next to Angolo Primary School in Northern Uganda.

Think about whether the writer's facts could be checked. Where could you look to check the facts on Ryan's story?

←

←

Look for names of established organizations and public figures. What connections do you find to Ryan's story?

Angolo Primary School

Look for evidence the writer has carefully researched the topic. What do you learn on this page that helps you understand the problem Ryan wants to solve?

The closest water source to the school was a swamp 5 km away. Many of the children had large, extended bellies from infestations of intestinal worms. At any given time, nearly a quarter of the students had diarrhea. Typhoid and other deadly water-borne diseases were also common. With no doctors in the area that is home to 31 850 people, one in five children died before age 5.

Ryan listened intently as Gizaw explained the slow process of building a well with a hand auger—a task requiring 20 people working for 10 days or more. "Drilling equipment would allow us to make many more wells," he said. He already knew the type he wanted—a small drill that could be transported in the back of a truck. It would cost $25 000.

"I'll raise the money for that drill," Ryan said quietly. "I want everyone in Africa to have clean water."

Back home, Susan told Mark, "We're raising money for a $25 000 well drill now." Mark's face dropped. He believed they were setting Ryan up for failure.

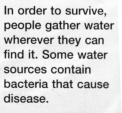
In order to survive, people gather water wherever they can find it. Some water sources contain bacteria that cause disease.

Ryan's Well

Part 2

Susan wrote to one of the *Citizen's* editors, telling him about Ryan's meeting with WaterCan and asking when Derek's article would be published. The editor called her back. "It'll be in tomorrow's paper."

When it appeared the next day, an Ottawa TV station called, wanting to interview Ryan. Newspapers across Canada reprinted the story.

A week later a letter arrived in the Hreljacs' mailbox, addressed to "Ryan's Well, Kemptville, Ontario." Inside was a cheque for $25 and a note saying, "I wish I could do more."

Shortly after, another cheque came in, this time addressed to Ryan's Well, Holy Cross School. It was for $20. After seeing Ryan's story on television, a group of Eastern Ontario well drillers gave Ryan $2700 for his cause.

Within two months, the little boy had inspired $7000 in donations.

By now Ryan's Grade 2 friends were clamouring to help. Their teacher, Lynn Dillabaugh, had never seen a child inspire others so much.

Applying Strategies

Evaluating

As you read, remember to evaluate the text by drawing conclusions about the validity of the ideas and information:

- Look for evidence that the writer has carefully researched the topic.
- Determine if the writer presents a clear point of view that matches the facts.
- Look for names of established organizations and public figures.
- Think about whether the writer's facts could be checked.

Ryan meets Walter, the well driller who convinced other drillers to donate money to Ryan's cause.

This is Jimmy at about the time he first wrote to Ryan.

Lynn informed parents that the class wished to raise money for another well and placed a watering can in the classroom for her students to drop coins in. She also asked WaterCan to help her start a pen-pal relationship with Angolo Primary. CPAR-Uganda offered to deliver the letters and pick up the Ugandan children's replies.

The first batch of letters went off in January 1999. Two months later a package from Angolo arrived with letters addressed to each student. Ryan was handed his, the large print filling the page:

Dear Ryan, my name is Akana Jimmy. I am 8 years old. I like soccer. Our house is made of grass. How is America? Your friend, Akana Jimmy.

With the letter was a photograph of Jimmy taken by CPAR. For weeks Ryan raved about his new pen pal. Could he meet him? he asked. Susan and Mark thought they might be able to afford a trip one day. Perhaps when Ryan was 12.

Ryan wrote back:

Dear Jimmy, It must be cool to have a house made out of grass. I am 8 now. Do you drink from my well every day? What is your favourite subject in school? I am going to Uganda when I am 12. My house is made out of bricks. Write back soon. Your friend, Ryan.

Backed now by the entire school, Ryan continued fundraising. He spent hours hand-printing letters, and asking organizations for money for his drill. When donations came in, he wrote thank-you notes. By November he had collected enough for CPAR-Uganda to buy the new machinery.

Shortly before Christmas Bruce Paynter, the Hreljacs' neighbour, asked his wife what she wanted as a present. "I don't really need anything," Bev Paynter replied. "But I'd love for Ryan to be able to go see his well."

Soon after, Bruce, a frequent air traveller, presented Ryan and his parents with air miles to help get them to Uganda, and when the *Ottawa Citizen* published a request for more air-mile donations, the community quickly responded. WaterCan also donated to the family's airfare and other travel expenses.

• • •

On the hot morning of July 27, 2000, a truck bearing Gizaw, Ryan, and his parents bumped its way down a Ugandan dirt road. As it neared Angolo, four tiny children spotted them and began jumping up and down excitedly. "Ryan! Ryan! Ryan!" they called.

"They know my name!" Ryan cried in surprise.

"Everybody for a hundred kilometres knows your name, Ryan," Gizaw said.

Around a bend, a line of some 5000 children from nearby schools stood waiting along the roadside. As the truck approached, they began clapping in a rhythmic beat.

"Let's get out," Gizaw said.

Children pump water from Ryan's well.

His head down, Ryan walked by the clapping children, waving bashfully. A band formed before them and, to music, led the procession to Angolo Primary School.

There, village elders greeted Ryan solemnly and took him to his well beside the school's vegetable garden. Adorned with flowers, the well had a message etched in the concrete base:

Ryan's Well:
Formed by Ryan Hreljac
For Community of Angolo
Primary School

Akana Jimmy, a tall, thin boy, much like Ryan, stood waiting by the well for his pen pal.

"Hello," Jimmy said shyly.

"Hi, Jimmy," Ryan replied. They stood together awkwardly, uncomfortable with the attention on them. Then Jimmy grabbed Ryan's hand and led him to the well so that he could cut the ribbon. Later, with Ryan's parents, they walked to some chairs set up in a field.

An elder stood up. "Look around at our children," he said. "You can see they're healthy. This is because of Ryan and our friends in Canada. For us, water is life."

A high-pitched wail came from the crowd. The headmaster, holding a small goat, stepped out and placed the squealing animal next to Ryan. "A gift of appreciation from Angolo," he said, bowing. Ryan cupped his hands over his mouth in delight, while Susan and Mark were presented with gifts of wood carvings and pottery.

Two dozen boys erupted from the crowd and, in a circle, began performing a traditional hunting dance to the sound of drums. Ryan laughed excitedly as Jimmy took his hand and led him outside the circle. Then Jimmy jumped in, and as Ryan followed, everyone cheered.

Ryan and Jimmy finally meet.

Dancers entertain Ryan and his family at the celebration to open Ryan's well.

Ryan attends school with Jimmy at Angolo School.

After four hours of dancing and celebration, Susan got up to speak. "I just want to say," she said, tears in her eyes, "that this has been the happiest day of my life. It will live in my heart forever."

That night, noticing Ryan was very quiet, Susan asked how he was feeling. "I feel wonderful, Mom," he said. Susan gave her son a hug, and together they began to recite their bedtime ritual: "Star light, star bright, the first star I see tonight..." And then Ryan rounded off that unforgettable day with his nightly prayer: "I wish for everyone in Africa to have clean water."

Since Angolo Primary School and the community began using Ryan's well for their cooking and drinking water, the rates of diarrhea and water-borne disease have dropped.

In 2001, Ryan's family helped him form the Ryan's Well Foundation. The foundation's mission is "to inspire, motivate, and empower children and adults to share Ryan's vision of a world where everyone has clean water." As of 2006, the foundation had built 245 wells in 11 different countries, bringing clean water to almost 400 000 people.

Reflect on

Strategies: What conclusions did you draw as you evaluated this text? What helped you reach your conclusions?

Critical Literacy: How would this article change if it were told from Jimmy's point of view?

Distinguishing between Revising and Editing

You know that writing is a process. You begin by gathering ideas. Next, you write a draft to get your ideas on paper. Then, you revise, edit, and create a good copy.

Sometimes, the revising and editing stages seem to be the same because you're "fixing" your draft. But these stages are very different. Read Jordan's draft, revised draft, and good copy. Think about why revising and editing are two different stages in the writing process.

rotary (first draft)
by Jordan

My mom is a member of rotary. Rotary is an international organization. Rotary promotes humanitarian service and goodwill and peace in the world. I got interested in rotary when mom told me about polio. Rotary is a leader in the Global Polioo Eradication Initiative and is the largest private doner. It has contributed over 600 million. Polio isterrible. It's prime target is children under 3. before the campane to wipe out polio, polio paralyzed more then 1 000 children a day. Today polio declined by 99%. Today, polio is stil a danger to children in Nigeria, India, Pakistan, and Afghanistan. Vaksinations can prevent polio easily A child can be protected for less than one dollar. Rotarians have delivered vaksines by camels, helicopters, trucks, and motorbikes. I made my personal contribution to polio I want to live in a world that is polio-free. Don't you.

Dreaming of a polio free world (revised draft)
by Jordan

Show that you care. Those four words kept whispering in my head but I didn't know what to do. my mom gave me the inspiration I needed. She's a member of rotary, an international organization that promotes humanitarian service. Rotary is a leader in the Global Polio Eradication Initiative.

Polio is a cruel disease. It targets children under 3 and can paralyze them. before the campane to wipe out polio began in 1988 polio paralyzed more then 1000 children a day. Today polio declined by 99%. The bad news is that polio is stil very common in Nigeria, India, Pakistan, and Afghanistan. Yet less than a dollar worth of vaksine can easily protect a child against polio. Rotarians have delivered vaksines by camels, helicopters, trucks, and motor bikes.

Volunteers are esential but a problem this size takes money to solve. Rotary has contributed over 600 million. I now contribute 25% of my allowance every week. I want to live in a polio-free world. Don't you.

Dreaming of a Polio-free World
by Jordan

Show that you care. Those four words kept whispering in my head, but I didn't know what to do. My mom gave me the inspiration I needed. She's a member of Rotary, an international organization that promotes humanitarian service. Rotary is a leader in the Global Polio Eradication Initiative.

Polio is a cruel disease. It targets children under three and can paralyze them. Before the campaign to wipe out polio began in 1988, polio paralyzed more than 1000 children a day. Today, polio has declined by 99%. The bad news is that polio is still very common in Nigeria, India, Pakistan, and Afghanistan. Yet less than a dollar's worth of vaccine can easily protect a child against polio. Rotarians have delivered vaccines by camels, helicopters, trucks, and motor bikes!

Volunteers are essential, but a problem this size takes money to solve. Rotary has contributed over $600 million. I now contribute 25% of my allowance every week. I want to live in a polio-free world. Don't you?

How to distinguish between revising and editing:

Revising

☑ Read your draft aloud and think about how to make it stronger.

☑ Make leads more interesting, improve the flow of ideas, and make better word choices.

☑ Add or delete information to make your message stronger.

Editing

☑ Read your draft aloud to check for problems.

☑ Correct errors in spelling, punctuation, and grammar.

Understanding text patterns

Identifying Characteristics of Problem-and-Solution Text Pattern

Writers often use problem-and-solution text pattern when they want readers to think about issues and challenges facing our society. Problem-and-solution text pattern has certain characteristics:

- An important problem, or issue, is presented.
- The problem is explored.
- One or more solutions is suggested.

An important problem, or issue, is presented. What problem did Dr. Stirling identify?

Solving the Puzzle of GLOBAL WARMING

by Maisie Park

POLAR BEARS AND ARCTIC ICE

Biologist Dr. Ian Stirling has been studying polar bears in the Arctic for 35 years. About 20 years ago, he began to notice that the bears were thinner and sicker than in previous years, and there were fewer cubs. The polar bears were in trouble—but why?

Dr. Stirling knew that polar bears eat ring seals *only* out on the ice, mainly from May to early July. He also knew that the ice was breaking up earlier than it had in the past. Dr. Stirling began keeping records and comparing ice break-up times with the condition of the polar bears. He found his answer. Generally, the earlier the ice broke up, the less time bears had to hunt for ring seals. Less food for the bears led to health problems and the birth of fewer cubs. But this answer raised a new question. Why was the ice breaking up earlier?

Polar bears only hunt ring seals before the ice breaks up.

The problem is explored. What did Dr. Stirling learn?

Other scientists had also been reporting changes in the Arctic ice. The ice was getting thinner and there was less of it. In some parts of Antarctica, the situation was the same. Could the polar regions, or maybe even the whole planet, be getting warmer?

GLOBAL WARMING— WHAT'S THE BIG PROBLEM?

Global warming isn't new. Temperatures on Earth have varied many times during our planet's long history. Periods of cold, with ice covering much of the planet, have been followed by periods of warmth. These cycles of warm and cold can last for millions of years. Maybe the changes scientists were noticing in the polar regions were just the effects of the beginning of a new warming period.

One thing we do know is that Earth's surface temperature has averaged about 15 °C for a long time. We can thank the greenhouse effect for that. Certain gases in the atmosphere act like the glass in a greenhouse and trap some of the Sun's heat. Otherwise, the heat would bounce off Earth and travel back into space. Without these greenhouse gases, Earth would be just another cold rock in space. But what would happen if Earth got warmer than it is now?

← An important problem, or issue, is presented. What new problem did Dr. Stirling and other scientists begin to consider?

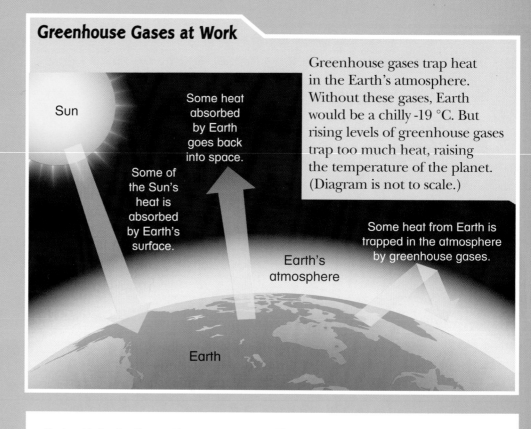

Greenhouse Gases at Work

Sun

Some heat absorbed by Earth goes back into space.

Some of the Sun's heat is absorbed by Earth's surface.

Earth's atmosphere

Some heat from Earth is trapped in the atmosphere by greenhouse gases.

Earth

Greenhouse gases trap heat in the Earth's atmosphere. Without these gases, Earth would be a chilly -19 °C. But rising levels of greenhouse gases trap too much heat, raising the temperature of the planet. (Diagram is not to scale.)

Scientists believe that a warmer Earth would show symptoms such as these:

- Plants and animals that commonly live in southern regions would be found living and breeding in northern regions.

- Hurricane activity would be more intense, with stronger winds and more rainfall.

- Other extreme weather events such as heat waves, drought, flooding, and wildfires would become more common.

- Mountain glaciers would show distinct signs of melting.

We are already seeing signs of these and similar events. But to tie them to global warming, scientists needed to know why they were happening in the first place.

Warmer temperatures and drought make forests drier and more likely to catch fire.

SOLVING THE GLOBAL WARMING MYSTERY

Why is Earth heating up? This was the mystery that scientists set out to solve.

In 1958, researcher Charles Keeling began measuring carbon dioxide in the atmosphere. Carbon dioxide is a gas that we breathe out. It is also released when we cut down and burn forests or use fossil fuels such as oil, gas, and coal. It is one of the most important greenhouse gases.

Keeling's measurements show that the amount of carbon dioxide in the atmosphere has been rising steadily each decade. Why? Since the start of the 20th century, fuel-burning industries have been increasing in size and number. Vast areas of forest have been cleared, and huge amounts of polluting gases have been pumped into the atmosphere. The amount of other greenhouse gases has also been growing.

Scientists began to ask questions. Were the gases we were putting into the atmosphere causing global warming? As the amount of these gases increased, were they holding in more of the Sun's heat, causing Earth's temperature to rise? At first there was an intense debate. No, said some scientists—the rising temperatures are just part of a natural cycle. But as more and more evidence was gathered, the majority of scientists came to agree that human activities are responsible for the rising levels of greenhouse gases, and these gases are causing global warming.

An important problem, or issue, is presented. What information does the writer provide to help you understand the problem?

All over the world, forests are being cut down. Trees absorb carbon dioxide—a greenhouse gas—from the air.